HEIRLOOM COOKBOOK

Recipes Handed Down by ~~Jothers~~
and Modern Recipes from D ~~Frie~~

KAR-BE
PUBLISH

PREFACE

Heirlooms come in many forms, shapes, and designs. Characteristically, all of them possess inherent value and sentimental worth, usually embracing fond memories.

Recipes that won the hearts of those who experienced them, on various occasions, especially birthday celebrations, holidays, and anniversaries, involving family and friends, may very well take on heirloom status.

Keeping alive these simple treasures is the purpose of *Heirloom Cookbook.* May the recipes it contains add to the enjoyment at many tables on many occasions.

Compiled and edited by
Miriam Lerner Satz

ACKNOWLEDGMENTS

Heirloom Cookbook was first conceived when my teenage niece, Leah Lerner, asked about her maternal
Hamantashen recipe. Her father, soc

the many recipes I had been collecting and to organize them into this book.

I am deeply grateful to my mother, the late Lena Lerner chwartz, my mother-in-law, the late Bertha Satz, our Leah or earnestly seeking an answer to her culinary question, and my brother, Harry Lerner, who encouraged the writing of this book and publishing it.

— *Miriam Lerner Satz*

n Data

wn by Jewish mothers and modern recipes from ed by Miriam Lerner Satz.— Rev. and expanded.

r)

CONTENTS

Section I
Lerner and Satz Family Recipes   4

Section II
Recipes from Miriam Lerner Satz   34

Section III
Passover Recipes   81

Section IV
Sephardic (Spanish Jewish) Cooking   87

Section V
Favorite Recipes from Friends   93

SECTION I

Lerner and Satz Family Recipes

Recipes from Lena Lerner

Flooden
Lena Lerner
Lena Lerner's favorite Purim dessert

1 cup honey
1 cup sugar
½ cup small noodle squares (Kosher)
big package of nuts (walnuts)

Brown noodle squares in oven but watch that it is not too brown. Put all ingredients together and boil until it looks like jam. Cool in double boiler and keep warm water in bottom of pan. Fill Ritz crackers or other cookies (shortbread type) with mixture (like a sandwich). Work with cold water on hands. *Great Purim dessert.*

Snowflakes
Lena Lerner

2 eggs
1 teaspoon sugar
½ teaspoon salt
flour

Beat eggs, sugar, and salt together. Add flour little by little until it gets thick like dumplings. Roll out on floured board and cut into strips. Fry in deep fat and sprinkle with powdered sugar through sifter.
Delicious!

Marshmallow Candy
Lena Lerner

2 squares baking chocolate
1 egg
1½ cups small colored or white marshmallows
2 tablespoons butter
1 cup powdered sugar
1 cup nuts

Melt butter. Add powdered sugar, chocolate, and egg. Mix well. Cook on stove until thick. Cool a little. Add marshmallows and mix together. Spread out on wax paper and add colored or white coconut. Cool and cut into squares.

Kamesh Bread
Lena Lerner

2 eggs
¾ cup sugar
¼ cup Canola or Mazola oil
3 tablespoons warm water
¼ cup raisins
¼ cup chopped nuts
1 teaspoon vanilla
pinch of salt
1¼ cups flour
1 teaspoonful of cocoa
1 teaspoon baking powder

Mix shortening with sugar. Add large eggs and mix well one at a time. Add 3 tablespoons warm water, vanilla, salt. Sift flour with baking powder. Add to mixture. Then add nuts and raisins. Take off couple, 3 tablespoons of mixture, and put aside. Take 1 teaspoon cocoa and add to mixture. Grease pan with oil. Put in half batter. Add chocolate layer. Add rest of batter. Swirl batter with knife. Bake in 325° oven for 45 minutes. Test with toothpick.

Kicklach (Puffy Egg Cookies)
Lena Lerner

½ cup oil
4 large eggs
2 cups flour
pinch of salt
2 full teaspoons sugar

Mix oil, eggs, sugar together on mixer. Add salt and flour gradually (¼ at a time). If too loose, add more flour, if too thick add less flour. Mix for a few minutes on speed 2 or 3. Fold with spatula until smooth. Full teaspoon of dough on greased pan. Bake for 20 minutes. Don't open oven. Bake more if necessary. Keep in oven with door closed for another 20 minutes to dry out. 375° oven.

Honey Cake
Lena Lerner

1 egg
½ cup sugar
½ cup honey
¾ cup boiled water or coffee (warm)
¼ cup Mazola oil
2¼ cups flour
1 teaspoon baking powder
½ teaspoon soda
½ cup nuts
½ teaspoon salt
½ cup raisins

Put egg, sugar, water, honey, oil, flour; all ingredients into mixing bowl. Set at 6 or 7 speed and mix until smooth. Bake 40 minutes or longer. 325° oven. Test.

Jelly Roll
Lena Lerner

2 eggs
¾ cup sugar
½ cup shortening
½ cup oil (Mazola)
¼ cup cold water
½ teaspoon salt
1 teaspoon vanilla
3½ cups flour
2 teaspoons baking powder
½ cup nuts, raisins, jam

Cream shortening with sugar, then add oil. Then add eggs one at a time and beat. Sift flour with baking powder. Add salt. Knead. Makes 2 rolls. Roll out, put jelly, nuts, and raisins and roll. Sometimes put oil on the board. Leave end of roll without jelly. Grease pan with shortening. Use 350° oven and bake until golden brown, 45 minutes.

Jelly Roll (Sponge)
Lena Lerner

2 eggs
¾ cup sugar
½ cup warm water from kettle
3 tablespoons oil
1¼ cup flour (bread)
1 teaspoon baking powder
½ teaspoon vanilla

Grease pan real well. Beat eggs with sugar, add ½ cup water and oil. Sift flour with baking powder and add. Put dough in long pan. Bake 30 minutes in 350° oven. Wet towel and sprinkle with powdered sugar. Jelly roll quite soft. Cut dough on towel. Spread jam and roll. Let stay on wet towel for a few minutes.

Bread Rolls
Lena Lerner

1 dry package of yeast
1½ sifter of flour
¼ cup Mazola oil
¼ cup shortening (or less)
¼ cup sugar (or less)
1 teaspoon salt
1 cup warm water (½ at a time)
1 egg, beaten
1 tablespoon water
poppy seeds

Mix up with hole in the middle of dish. Let spoon come out dry. Let rise for 1 hour. One teaspoon oil on top. Make cloverleaf rolls. Roll in little flour 3 pieces and place together. Mix beaten egg with water and brush on top and add poppy seeds. 325°–350° oven 30 minutes or more.

Sweet Rolls
Lena Lerner

1 package yeast
1 sifter flour
2 eggs
1 cup sugar
½ cup Mazola oil
1 cup half milk and water
½ cup shortening

Dissolve yeast in warm water—3 tablespoons. Add all ingredients. Don't knead too hard. Add raisins and cinnamon. Use no flour but oil on board for rolling out the dough. Add more flour if needed. Use 325–350° oven for 30 minutes or more.

Cheese Bagalach
Lena Lerner

2 cups flour
¾ cup warm water from faucet
¼ teaspoon salt
2 teaspoons Mazola oil

Step #1:
Knead dough. Sift flour, add oil, salt, take ½ cup warm water then ¼ cup and mix with wooden spoon. Spread flour on board and knead 2 leaves. Roll out by using rolling pin. Place two leaves between two towels and put in refrigerator for 1 hour or 1¼ hour. Take out top towel and flour it and put on counter. Put Turkish towel on bottom. Take leaves out and put on towel and cover with bottom towel. Let stand for 1 hour or 1½ hours.

Step #2:
Sprinkle flour on tablecloth. Roll leaves a little, then stretch by hand. Take off ends and spread 1 drop of melted margarine or Mazola oil. Put one layer of filling on leaf and roll, like a jelly roll. Dot leaves with butter. Bake in 350° oven for 30 minutes or longer. Cut in 4-inch pieces while warm.

Filling variations for Cheese Bagalach:

Cheese
1 container of dry cottage cheese;
  squeeze out water
1 egg
1 teaspoon salt
2 teaspoons sugar
1 teaspoon cracker crumbs.
Knead well and use as filling for Bagalach.

Buckwheat Grits
Cook grits according to directions. Add fried onions (soft). Salt onions before frying and then cover. Add chicken fat and mix well. Taste. Pinch of pepper.

Potato
Cook peeled potatoes with salt. Drain and put back on fire and mash well. Add fried onions or chopped griven and mix until real fine. Add chicken fat to potatoes and mash. Taste.

Rice
1 cup rice to 2½ cups water
Cook over direct flame for 3 minutes then in double boiler for 15 minutes. Add 3 tablespoons sugar, add 1 tablespoon margarine, 1 egg, 1 teaspoon salt, ¼ cup milk and mix well and use as filling.

Honey Cake #2
Lena Lerner

½ cup oil (Mazola)
3 eggs
1 cup honey
1 cup sugar
1 cup chopped nuts
1 cup coffee-warm (not strong)
1 teaspoon soda mixed into coffee
1 teaspoon baking powder in 3½ cups flour
  (more or less)
pinch of salt

Mix oil, sugar, honey, and eggs. Add baking powder to flour and mix alternately with coffee. Add chopped nuts. Grease loaf pans and bake in 350° oven for 1 hour.
Makes 2 loaves

7

Noodle Pudding
Lena Lerner

½ package noodles
1 egg
1 teaspoon chicken fat
1 teaspoon sugar
dash of pepper

Cook noodles in salt water according to directions. Beat all ingredients together. Grease pan and bake in 350° oven for 45 minutes or longer.

Rice Pudding
Lena Lerner

1 cup rice
1 egg
1 teaspoon chicken fat
¼ cup sugar
½ lemon not strained
¼ cup raisins
little cinnamon

Cook rice and add rest of ingredients. Mix well. Grease pan. Use 350° oven for 25 minutes or longer.

Famous Cheese Rolls
Lena Lerner

2 egg yolks
2 teaspoons baking powder
½ cup shortening
½ cup sour cream
¼ cup warm water
2 cups flour
⅛ teaspoon salt

Mix all ingredients together and refrigerate for several hours.

Cheese Filling:
2 small containers of pot cottage cheese
3 eggs
1 tablespoon sour cream
2 teaspoons sugar
pinch of salt

Mix all ingredients. Make two rolls out of dough. Roll out on wax paper. Place filling in center and around edges. Roll as for jelly roll. Place in greased baking dish and bake in a 375° oven for 45 minutes to 1 hour or until well browned. Slice and serve with sour cream. Can be wrapped in foil and frozen to be heated later in the oven.

Pesach Popovers
Lena Lerner

½ cup oil
1 teaspoon sugar (optional)
2 cups cold water
1 cup matzo meal
3 eggs
1 teaspoon salt

Mix oil, salt, sugar, and water and have it come to a boil. Then add cup of matzo meal and stir until spoon comes out clean. Cool. Add 3 eggs, one at a time and beat well. Put in greased muffin pans and bake in 400° oven for 30 minutes or longer.

Kneidlach (Matzo Balls)
Lena Lerner

1 cup matzo meal
3 tablespoons chicken fat
½ teaspoon salt
½ cup cold water
2 well-beaten eggs

Mix all ingredients together and form into balls. Place in boiling water and cook for 20 minutes.

Pesach Meeana (Liver Dish)
Lena Lerner

1 pound liver or a little less
4 eggs
½ salt
¼ cup cold water
1 cup matzo meal

Broil liver and grind with griven. Add eggs and beat. Add ¼ cup water, salt, and pepper. Add 1 cup matzo meal and mix. Add small amount of chicken fat and grease pan with same. Place some fat on top and bake in 375° oven for 30 minutes or longer.

Meat and Dairy Dishes

Mamaliga—Cheese and Butter
Lena Lerner

1½ cups cornmeal
3 cups cold water
1 teaspoon salt
melted butter or margarine
cottage cheese

Mix cornmeal, cold water, and salt together. Cook mixture in a large pot and stir continuously until it thickens. Makes a pretty large amount. Take a spoonful of mamaliga, dip in melted butter or margarine and then dip in cottage cheese. A favorite of the Lerner family.
Enjoy!

Hamburger Patties
Lena Lerner's Specialty

1 or 2 pounds of ground beef
1 egg for each pound
2 to 4 tablespoons cracker meal or matzo meal
¼ cup cold water
salt, pepper, garlic

Mix all ingredients together and form into thick patties. Fry in oil in skillet and then transfer to a baking dish and place in 350° oven for about 30 minutes or until done.
Delicious!

Kreplach
Lena Lerner

2 cups flour
½ cup cold water
1 egg

Sift flour, add egg and water. Make a stiff dough. Roll out on floured board.

Filling:
less than ½ pound dry cottage cheese
1 egg
¼ teaspoon salt

Mix ingredients real well with fork. Roll dough thin and cut into shape (rectangles). Add filling and paste well, then turn corners. Use flour for pasting.

Boil water ⅔ pan full and add 2 tablespoons salt. Throw kreplach in one by one. When done take out and put in strainer and let water drip out. Fry in margarine.

Cottage Cheese Dumplings
Lena Lerner

½ dry cottage cheese container
1 egg
salt to taste
little sugar
matzo meal just to thicken

Mix all ingredients. Boil water with salt. Make dumplings and cook for 10 minutes. Serve with sour cream.

Eggplant Appetizer
Lena Lerner

1 eggplant
1 tablespoon oil
¼ cup onion, diced or minced
season with salt, pepper, and garlic salt
¼ cup green pepper, diced (optional)

Wash eggplant and prick with fork. Place in aluminum pie pan and broil in oven, turning occasionally, until well done, around 15 minutes. Remove from oven and immediately run cold water over the eggplant until it cools. Peel and chop with hand chopper or use fork. Add oil, onions, and green pepper. Season with salt, pepper, and garlic salt to taste. Refrigerate for several hours. Serve over lettuce as an appetizer or as a side vegetable dish.

Cottage Cheese Pudding
Lena Lerner

½ package medium noodles
3 tablespoons sugar
2 eggs
½ pound dry cottage cheese
1 tablespoon melted butter
½ cup sour cream

Cook noodles in salted water. Drain. Rinse through cold water—not too much. Beat eggs with sugar. Add noodles, cheese, melted butter, sour cream, and 1 teaspoon salt. Mix well. Grease pan and use 350° oven for 30 minutes or longer. Serve with sour cream.

Chicken Fat
Lena Lerner

Wash fat and cut in little pieces. Put on a small fire and let it boil until griven come on top. Mix. Cut up onion and put in fat. Cook until onions are brown. Strain. Keep griven separate and covered. Place in refrigerator.

Chopped Liver
Lena Lerner

Scald liver. Broil liver and then grate on large side of grater. Also grate in 1 onion. Cut celery in small pieces. Chop in hard-cooked egg (add tomatoes if no egg). Chop well.

Liver Patties
Lena Lerner

Use raw egg in grated liver and add 1 teaspoon cracker crumbs or matzo meal. Drop by tablespoon into pan and broil until done.

Oatmeal Pancakes
Lena Lerner

You cook the oatmeal as if you were making cereal and if any is left over, you take 2 eggs, beat it with the oatmeal. If it is too thick, take a very little milk or cream and mix up with a little flour, just enough to make pancakes, but don't make it too soft; otherwise, it will not keep its shape. Fry in oil.

Cabbage Soup
Lena Lerner

You take a small head of cabbage and slice it into very small pieces. Put some salt in and rub it first and wash it in hot water, and put in a sliced onion and a piece of meat and put on stove and brown for awhile. Then put some warm water, as much as you think you need, pour in a can of tomato soup and 1 lemon strained or 1½ lemons to help make it sour and sweet by adding some sugar.

Beet Borscht
Lena Lerner

6 medium beets (parboil, peel and use food processor, shredded)
3 rhubarbs or 2 lemons (keep out of refrigerator so they will be more juicy)
½ cup sugar
1 tablespoon salt
1 egg
(with meat use 1 whole onion)

Peel beets and slice. Add 2 quarts cold water or more. Put on stove and then cut up leaves, rhubarb, and salt. Let soup come to a boil for at least 5 minutes or more, add sugar (or lemon if necessary) to taste. After beets are cooked mix 1 beaten egg with salt and add small amount of borscht to beaten egg. Beat well and then put into soup. Serve cold.

Cabbage Borscht
Lena Lerner

Add cabbage cut into strips when water begins to boil. Put meat, beets in at the beginning but no egg. Cook as long as needed.

Buckwheat Grits
Lena Lerner

Heat grits (¾ to 1 cup) until hot. Add 1 teaspoon salt. Stir. When hot, add boiling water (2 cups). Cover and turn on low flame for 10 minutes.

Chicken Soup
Lena Lerner

1 chicken, cut in pieces
4 quarts cold water
2 carrots, quartered
2 stalks celery and celery tops
1 sprig parsley
1 sprig dill
1 whole onion
1 whole peeled parsnip (optional)
1 tablespoon salt or more to taste

Clean pieces of chicken and place in large soup kettle. Add cold water to rim of pan. Add large onion and peeled parsnip. Cook uncovered until soup comes to a slow boil. Spoon off skim that has formed on top.

Add salt, carrots, celery, and celery top. Cover and cook for 2 hours or longer. Add parsley and dill toward end of cooking time. Remove chicken. If desired, cover chicken with corn flake crumbs and roast at 325° for 20 minutes or until chicken is crispy. Serve soup with cooked rice, egg barley, or noodles.

Variation:
Can add 2 whole peeled potatoes to soup but take out before they start to get too soft. Mother always did this in her later years.

Canned Beet Borscht
Lena Lerner

1 can beets—diced or shredded
1½ cans cold water
1 lemon
little salt, pepper, and garlic salt
sugar to taste
1 egg yolk
cream

Cook beets and water for 5 to 10 minutes. Add 1 lemon strained and seasonings. Cool off and mix beaten egg yolk with cream. Put in borscht. Add butter if cream not rich enough. Use no milk.

Rolled Roast
Lena Lerner

Place roast in pan. Put crushed garlic on roast and on bottom of pan. Add salt, pepper, and paprika. Uncovered. Put in 350° oven. When meat begins to brown, put in ½ cup warm water and put on top of meat. If dry, baste again.

Roast Turkey or Chicken
Lena Lerner

Crush clove of garlic with salt and rub all over chicken or turkey inside and out. Stuff.
Put chopped onions in roasting pan.
Add chicken or turkey. Baste with gravy.
Add water if necessary. Use 325° oven 2 hours or longer.

Roast Beef
Lena Lerner

Cut onion in pieces. Rub meat with crushed garlic, salt, and paprika. Place meat on top of onions. Cook over low flame and cover. After 15 or 20 minutes, turn over. Cook over 2 hours. When onions are brown, add a little warm water from kettle. Test with knife or fork until tender. Cool and slice.

Roast Chicken with Rice
Lena Lerner

Rub chicken with garlic, salt, pepper, and paprika. Place in 350° oven without rack. Put onions in after chicken has been in for ½ hour. Baste with warm water from faucet. Turn chicken and reduce oven to 325°. After awhile put in 2 cups rice (plain) in one corner and chopped onions in the other side. Add 1 or more teaspoons salt, sprinkle over rice, and roast until rice is brown. Put water from kettle over rice to cover and mix onions with rice. Cover pan and bake in 325° oven. Can add a few quartered potatoes at the side.
Bake until everything is done.

Procas (Stuffed Cabbage Leaves)
Lena Lerner

1 medium cabbage
½ onion
1 pound ground beef
1 egg
⅓ cup cold water
¼ teaspoon salt
3 tablespoons cracker crumbs or bread crumbs
2 tablespoons rice

½ onion for pan
½ cup brown sugar or less
juice of 1½ lemons
1 pint of strained tomatoes

Pull cabbage leaves off. Place in roasting pan or Dutch oven and cover with boiling water. Cook for a few minutes until soft. Turn leaves over and cook a little longer until soft enough, drain water. Brown onion in chicken fat until a little brown. Add to roasting pan.

Meat Mixture:
Mix water, egg, onion, rice, crumbs, salt with meat. Mix well. Fold cabbage leaves with meat over pan. (Roll straight, then tuck in ends and squeeze.) Add lemon juice and brown sugar and use high flame. Strain tomatoes. After 15 minutes, lower flame and add tomatoes. Cook covered 1¼ hours over low flame.

Chopped Onions in Mazola Oil
Lena Lerner

1 onion chopped
3 tablespoons Mazola oil
bread

Chop onion in bowl and add oil. Season with salt, pepper, and garlic salt. Use as a dip with bread. *Enjoy!*

Tea Kettle Tea
Lena Lerner

½ cup warm milk
½ cup hot tea

Mix. We drank this mixture when we were young and couldn't drink coffee.

Gefilte Fish
Lena Lerner

**3 pounds fish (grind with 1 medium onion); use 2
   or 3 different types of fish**
½ glass cold water
3 eggs
**1 tablespoon Matzo meal or more,
   if necessary**
salt and pepper to taste

Mix all ingredients with electric beater, no. 6 for 5 minutes or more. Cut up 1 medium onion and fry in oil in Dutch oven. Add cold water to middle of pan. Form fish into balls (oval shape). Cook over medium heat for 2½ hours, uncovered. Move pan back and forth while cooking so fish will separate. If desired, add sliced carrot, celery, and quartered potatoes. Add cold water to pot when other water boils down.

Tomato Sauce for Gefilte Fish
Lena Lerner

4 to 6 pieces of gefilte fish
2 cooked, sliced carrots
½ cup can green peas
1 can tomato soup or strained tomatoes
butter or margarine

Slice 2 cooked carrots. Mix ½ can of green peas and 1 can tomato soup or strained tomatoes. Place pieces of gefilte fish in baking dish. Pour sauce over the fish, and place a piece of butter or margarine over each piece. Bake in 350° oven for 40 minutes.

Frozen Vegetables with Gefilte Fish
Lena Lerner

Cook ⅓ package of mixed vegetables according to directions. Place 4 to 6 pieces of gefilte fish in baking dish. Pour mixed vegetables over fish. Dot pieces with butter or margarine. Bake in 350° oven for 30 minutes.

Easy Macaroni and Cheese Dish
Lena Lerner
No eggs or milk.

½ box elbow macaroni, cooked
1 tablespoon butter or oil
**4 ounces Longhorn cheese or cheddar cheese,
   cubed**

Melt butter or olive oil in skillet. Add cooked macaroni and cubed pieces of Longhorn cheese. Add salt and pepper to taste. Cook until cheese melts and macaroni crisps a bit.

Blintzes
Lena Lerner

2 eggs
¼ cup cold water
1 cup flour
pinch of salt
1 cup cold water

Beat eggs well, add ¼ cup water and beat again. Then sift flour over batter and beat until there are no lumps. Add salt. Add 1 cup cold water at the end and beat well. Make pan hot with margarine (6- to 8-inch skillet). Pour batter at one side and turn pan. Lift after a few minutes and turn over and place on a towel.

Filling:
1 pound pot or dry cottage cheese
1 teaspoon sugar
1 teaspoon salt
1 teaspoon cracker crumbs
2 eggs

Mix ingredients well. Place mixture on cheese leaves and fold. Fry in margarine or oil until brown. Freezes well.

Ground Beef with Macaroni
Lena Lerner

1 pound ground beef
½ package elbow macaroni
1 chopped onion
2 tablespoons Mazola oil
1 stalk celery chopped (optional)
salt and pepper

Cook macaroni according to directions. Sauté chopped onion with celery in oil in skillet. Add ground beef and cook until red disappears. Add cooked macaroni and seasonings to mixture. Cook until macaroni crisps a bit.

Kasha with Shell Macaroni
Lena Lerner

1 cup kasha
1 egg beaten
2 cups boiling water
1 teaspoon salt
½ package cooked shell macaroni
2 tablespoons oil

Mix kasha with beaten egg and salt in bowl. Heat oil in skillet and add kasha. Cook until kasha crisps a little—about 5 minutes. Add boiling water, cover and cook until water disappears—about 15 minutes. Stir cooked shell macaroni into kasha. (Use less kasha, if desired, and eat as a side dish with beef and gravy.)

Beef Soup with Navy Beans
Lena Lerner

1 pound beef cubes
1 marrow bone
½ package navy beans
3 quarts water
salt and pepper
1 carrot, sliced
1 celery, sliced
1 whole onion

Cover navy beans with water and let stand overnight. Drain water. Mix beef, bone, navy beans (optional, cook separately and add later), carrot, celery, and onion in water and cook until meat is done, about 2 or more hours.

Salmon Loaf
Lena Lerner

1 can pink salmon
3 eggs
¼ cup cold water
¼ cup matzo meal
1 chopped onion
1 stalk celery
¼ cup chopped green pepper
1 tablespoon oil

Take off skin and bones in salmon but leave juice. Sauté onions, celery, and green pepper (covered) in oil until soft. Sprinkle with paprika. Beat eggs first and then add rest of ingredients. Season with salt and pepper. Put in greased loaf pan in a 350° oven for 45 minutes.

Pea Soup with Beef
Lena Lerner

1 to 2 lbs. cubed beef
1 package green or yellow peas
1 chopped onion
2 chopped carrots
2 chopped celery stalks
parsley and dill
bay leaf
thyme
marjoram
1 or 2 whole potatoes
cooked rice (optional)
salt and pepper

Mix all ingredients and place in a large pot. Cover with 3 or 4 quarts of cold water. Take out potatoes after they are cooked and use separately. Strain soup and add cooked rice, if desired. *Freezes well.*

Recipes from Lerner Family

Favorite Chocolate Fudge
Marge Lerner

¼ pound (1 stick) butter or margarine
1 large (13-ounce) can of milk
4 cups sugar
1 cup nuts, if desired
1 tablespoon vanilla
18-ounce package semi-sweet
 chocolate pieces
1 jar marshmallow creme or fluff
 (or 2 cups marshmallows)

Place first 4 ingredients in kettle and stir. Soon as it begins to bubble, change heat to low. Simmer for 11 minutes. Keep the mixture boiling (5½ minutes for half recipe). Have ready in mixing bowl 18 ounces semi-sweet chocolate and 1 jar of marshmallow creme or fluff. Pour cooked mixture into mixing bowl and beat until the candy creams (3 or 4 minutes with electric beater). Add chopped nuts, if desired. Spread in buttered tin. Refrigerate for 24 hours. Cut after it gets cool but not too hard. Keep refrigerated.

Ice Cream Pie
Lena Lerner

1 package Jell-O (raspberry, cherry, etc.)
1 pint ice cream (strawberry-pecan crunch)
16 to 20 graham crackers
¼ cup softened margarine

Dissolve Jell-O in 1½ cups hot water. Jell until part done. Soften ice cream. Mix Jell-O and add ice cream. Crush graham crackers with ¼ cup margarine. Mix with fingers. Put in pan and fill with ice cream Jell-O. Crush 2 graham crackers and place on top. Refrigerate.

Creamy Pumpkin Soup
Sandy Davis

¼ cup butter or margarine
1 large onion, peeled and chopped
  (about ¾ cup)
½ teaspoon curry powder
1 16-ounce can pumpkin (2 cups)
  or fresh pumpkin (2 cups)
¼ teaspoon salt
2 cups half-and-half or whole milk
2½ cups chicken stock (parve)
  (dissolve 3 teaspoons chicken bouillon
  granules in 21/2 cups boiling water)
⅓ cup sour cream
⅛ teaspoon cinnamon
minced parsley

Melt butter or margarine in a medium-sized saucepan. Add the chopped onion and, stirring frequently, cook until soft but not brown. Add the curry powder and cook 1 to 2 minutes longer.

Place the curried onion in a food processor or electric blender. Add the pumpkin and salt, then process (or blend) until smooth. Add the half-and-half (or milk) and process again until smooth.

Pour the pumpkin mixture back into the saucepan and stir in the chicken stock. Heat the soup slowly over low heat, stirring occasionally. Meanwhile, stir the cinnamon and minced parsley into the sour cream.

Serve the soup steaming hot with a dollop of seasoned sour cream atop each bowl. Served with a crusty French bread, this would also be a good lunch.

Variation:
Follow the above recipe until done. Add a cup of cooked rice to the soup. Omit the cinnamon, minced parsley, and sour cream or add if you so desire.
Makes 6 servings

17

Noodle Pudding
Ethel "Toots" Lerner

1 pound wide noodles
1 quart buttermilk
4 eggs, beaten
½ cup sugar (optional)
¼ teaspoon salt
¼ pound butter

Cook and drain noodles. Add butter to melt in noodles. Add remaining ingredients and mix well. Place in greased 9 x 12 inch pan. Bake 350° for 45 minutes. Remove from oven and sprinkle topping over it. Return to oven and bake 350° for additional 30 minutes. Pudding freezes well.

Topping (optional):
1 cup brown sugar
1 cup cornflake crumbs
⅛ pound melted butter, enough to hold sugar and crumbs together

Place on noodle pudding and bake again for 30 minutes.

Marble Coffee Cake
Ethel "Toots" Lerner

3 cups flour
4 eggs
3 teaspoons baking powder
1 cup milk
1 cup shortening (½ butter)
½ teaspoon salt
2 teaspoons vanilla
1½ cups sugar

Cream sugar and shortening. Add eggs, one at a time, and beat well. Add milk and flour alternately after flour has been mixed with baking powder and salt. Add vanilla. Grease Angel Food cake pan well.

Marbleized process:
⅓ cup sugar
2 tablespoons cocoa
1 teaspoon cinnamon

Put small amount of batter into pan, sprinkle cocoa and sugar mixture over it, continue, ending with cocoa mixture. Cut through mixture with knife. Bake 1 hour at 350°—*freezes well!*

Apple Cake
Esther Lerner

½ cup oil (Wesson) creamed together with
¾ cup sugar
3 eggs, cream again
1 teaspoon vanilla
1 teaspoon almond flavor
pinch of salt
1¼ cups flour sifted together with
    1 teaspoon baking powder
8" or 9" size Pyrex pan. Grease well with margarine.
3 or 4 apples (Jonathon)

Cut peeled apples into wedges (8ths) or smaller. Mix 1 teaspoon cinnamon and 1 teaspoon sugar. Place on top of batter in dish. In addition, take cinnamon again, shake over the top. Bake in 350° oven for 45 minutes and no more. Test.

Spinach Kugel
Esther Lerner

12-ounce package thin noodles
4 eggs
½ package onion soup (Mrs. Grass)
1 package frozen spinach

Cook spinach a few minutes and drain.
Add rest of ingredients. Grease pan, 9" x 13" with margarine. Use 350° oven for 1 hour or longer. Slice the next day.

Kamesh Brot
Esther Lerner

6 eggs
1 cup sugar
1 cup Mazola oil
3 teaspoons baking powder
pinch of salt
½ cup orange juice (fresh)
6 cups flour or more
1 cup crushed nuts
1 teaspoon vanilla (optional)
jelly, nuts, and cherries

Mix all ingredients and roll out as for a jelly roll and add jelly, nuts, and cherries. Use 375° oven and bake 30 minutes or longer.

Mandel Bread
Esther Lerner

½ pound margarine
1¼ cups sugar
cream margarine and sugar together
3 tablespoons oil
2 teaspoons vanilla

1 teaspoon almond flavor
6 eggs
4 cups flour
2 teaspoons baking powder
a little salt
rolled nuts, about 1 cup

Heat oven to 350° and grease 2 cookie sheets. Mix all ingredients well and make 4 rolls. Place 2 rolls in each sheet and bake in oven for 35 minutes or until brown. Let stand about 20 minutes after baking and then cover with a clean dry towel for 10 minutes. Cut in slices. Place on baking sheets again on flat side to dry in oven for a few minutes.

Chocolate Chip Cookies
Esther Lerner

1 stick butter
1 stick margarine
½ cup brown sugar
½ cup granulated sugar
cream sugars together
1 tablespoon hot water
2¼ cups flour
1 teaspoon baking powder
¼ teaspoon salt
2 eggs
1 teaspoon vanilla
1 cup chocolate chips

After creaming both sugars, add rest of ingredients. Refrigerate overnight.
Bake in 350° oven for 8–10 minutes or until light brown.

Roast Brisket or Chuck Roast
Esther Lerner

One or two carrots sliced. (No celery or water.) Slice three onions and one garlic and add to roasting pan along with the sliced carrots. Add meat, cover, and bake in 350° oven until tender. (Do not cover if baking a standing rib roast.)

Mondel Bread
Lil Bell

4 eggs
¾ cup butter, melted
1 cup sugar
1 teaspoon vanilla
3 cups flour
1 heaping teaspoon baking powder
½ teaspoon salt
1½ cups chopped pecans

Mix sugar and butter together. Add 1 egg at a time. Add vanilla. Then add sifted dry ingredients, then nuts. Spoon into 3 rows on cookie sheet. Bake in 350° oven for 25–30 minutes or until brown. Let cool slightly, then slice and put under broiler on one side. When brown, turn and put under broiler the other side. Watch. *Enjoy!*

Hamentaschen & Flacht Dough
Lil Bell

1 cup sugar
1 teaspoon salt
¾ oil
3–4 eggs
5¼ cups flour

¼ cup orange juice
2 teaspoons baking powder
¼ cup milk (or additional orange juice)

Sift dry ingredients. Add together. Make well in center. Dump in all and eggs and mix dough. Put flour on top and let stand 2 hours. Roll out ½ to ¼ inches thick. Fill with apples-raisins, nuts or jelly, etc. Or roll out ⅛ inch thick and cut in rounds. Fill with hamentaschen filling. Bake in 325° oven for about 30 minutes.

Traditional Prune Filling:
Grind 1 pound prunes—pour boiling water over them. Let stand 5 to 10 minutes. Add 6 ounces walnuts and lemon juice to taste.

Chocolate Cake
Lil Bell

2 ounces chocolate
1 cup boiling water
½ cup shortening
Combine and stir until melted.

Add:
2 cups sugar less 1 tablespoon

Add:
2 cups cake flour mixed with ½ teaspoon salt and 1½ teaspoons baking soda

Add:
½ cup sour milk or buttermilk (can add glob of sour cream to make ½ cup sour milk)
2 unbeaten eggs

Grease and flour 9 x 13 pan. Line with wax paper. Bake at 325° oven for 25–30 minutes. Or make 20 cupcakes out of batter and use 350° oven 20 minutes or longer.

Chocolate Frosting
Lil Bell

¾ stick of margarine
3 cups powdered sugar
3 rounded tablespoons cocoa
pinch of salt
1 teaspoon vanilla
milk or cream

Mix all ingredients. Add milk or cream as
necessary.

Cherry Cream Pie
Sophie Braeman

9″ crust, baked
1 can Eagle brand condensed milk
⅓ cup lemon juice
1 teaspoon vanilla
½ teaspoon almond
½ pint whipping cream

Whip cream until stiff and fold into above
ingredients. Pour into baked shell. Top with 1 can
cherry pie filling. Chill for 3–4 hours or overnight
before cutting.

Pickles (Green Plum Tomatoes or Green Pickles)
Aunt Merle

Wash jars. In each pint jar on the bottom add:
1 small clove of garlic
1 small red pepper
½ teaspoon pickling spices
1 small bay leaf
1 flower and leaf of dill or ½ teaspoon dill seed
   and ½ teaspoon dill weed

Place pickles or tomatoes in jars until you cannot
add any more. In between add:

small sticks of carrots
small sticks of celery

On top add:
1 small garlic
½ teaspoon pickling spices

Salt solution add to each jar:
1 quart of cold water
3 tablespoons scant coarse salt or
   pickling salt

Pour until to the very top. Cover with a lid not
too tight and place in a jelly roll pan for 3 days.

After 3 days, remove cover, remove any
tomatoes or pickles that don't look good. Fill
again with more salt solution. Seal tightly. (Never
place dill on top but at the bottom because it
would be exposed to air and may spoil.)

Summer Squash, Sandwich Pickles
Ruth Goldberg

**5 quarts of summer squash
    (zucchini, etc., diced)
3 large onions, sliced
3 green peppers (large), sliced**

Place above ingredients in a large bowl.
Pour over the above 6 quarts of water and
1½ cups salt (pickling) and let set for
3 hours—drain. In a large pot add:
**5 pints of white vinegar
5 cups brown sugar
5 teaspoons mustard seed
2½ teaspoons celery seed
5 tablespoons pickling spices**

Tie together last 3 ingredients in spice bag. Bring
to a boil. Add peppers, onions, and squash and
bring to a boiling point again and discard spice
bag. Add 1 1/4 teaspoons turmeric. Pack in very
hot jars. Seal tightly.
Makes 12 pints

Givéch
Ada Wasserman
Cooked vegetable salad

**2 green peppers (or 1 yellow and 1 red for color)
    about 1 pound, cut into strips
3 large carrots, peeled and chopped
3 large onions, skinned and chopped
3 good tomatoes, cubed (peeled, if desired)
1¼ pound eggplant, in cubes but with skin on
1 tablespoon oil
¼ cup water
salt to taste**

Arrange in casserole in layers: carrots, peppers,
onion, with oil and water. Cook on top of stove
over medium heat. After about ½ hour, add
eggplant. Cook until liquid evaporates. During the
last 30 minutes of cooking, add tomatoes or 3
tablespoons ketchup. When it is cooked remove
from heat and spoon into a jar. Cool. Cover.
Refrigerate. Serve cold.

Roast Chicken
Esther Lerner

Place piece of aluminum foil in roasting pan. Slice
1 onion and put in pan. Add whole chicken or
pieces of chicken on top. Add seasoning. Cover
and bake in 350° oven until chicken is tender.

Variation:
Dip pieces of chicken in cornflake crumbs. Season
with salt and pepper. Bake uncovered in 350° oven
until chicken is tender.

Recipes from Mother Satz

Famous Poppy Seed Cookies
Mother Satz
*Makes great Hanukkah cookies because the dough
is easy to roll and cut.*

**4 cups flour
2 teaspoons baking powder
½ cup vegetable shortening
½ cup vegetable cooking oil
½ teaspoons salt
½ teaspoon vanilla
2 eggs
½ package or less of poppy seeds**

¼ **cup rolled nuts**
¼ **cup warm water from faucet**
¾ **or 1 cup sugar**

Sift flour with baking powder. Make a well in bowl. Put in poppy seeds, eggs, sugar, shortening, oil, salt, and vanilla. Knead. Roll out on a little flour. Grease pan. Cut cookies with small glass or Hanukkah cut-outs. Bake in 350° oven for 10 to 12 minutes.

Famous Meat Loaf
Mother Satz

2 pounds ground chuck
½ medium onion, grated
½ potato, grated
½ carrot, grated
2 eggs
1 teaspoon salt
dash of pepper
¼ cup water
2 to 4 tablespoons cracker meal
    (or bread crumbs)
½ onion, cut into pan (not mixed with
    other ingredients)
dash of garlic salt

Mix all ingredients together. Put cut onions on bottom of baking pan. Place meat loaf mixture in pan. Bake in 350° oven until well done, around 2 hours. Can form two loaves in pan, if preferred. Add quartered potatoes between the two loaves at same time so there is a meal in one pot.

Baked Beans
Mother Satz

2 cups navy or lima beans
1 onion
1 stalk celery
grated cheese or cut into pieces
3 tablespoons brown sugar
½ teaspoon salt
½ can of tomato soup

Cook beans in 4 cups cold water. Do not cook too tender. Fry onion, celery, salt, and pepper until soft. Grease a casserole dish and place beans in it and add onion and celery mixture and cheese and brown sugar to beans. Mix gently. Add tomato soup last. Bake in 350° oven for one-half hour.

Quick Baked Beans
Mother Satz

Cook 2 cups of beans in 4 cups water. Drain. Add ½ can of tomato soup, 2 tablespoons brown sugar and salt and pepper. Use a little margarine on top. Bake in 350° oven for 20 minutes.

Bread Stuffing
Mother Satz

1 cup bread crumbs
1 medium onion
1 stalk celery
¼ cup chopped green pepper
1 egg
½ teaspoon salt

Fry ½ onion, celery, and green pepper until soft. Put egg, ½ raw onion (grated), fried onion mixture, and pepper into bread crumbs. Mix well. Add ½ cup boiling water. Add 1 teaspoon chicken fat. Stuff chicken or turkey and bake in oven until done.

Taglach Dumplings
Mother Satz
Delicious in soups.

1 egg
salt and pepper
2 tablespoons cold water
flour

Beat egg well. Add 2 tablespoons cold water to egg. Add flour—not too thick or too loose. When soup is boiling, add small amount by spoon and cook until done.

Fillet of Sole
Mother Satz

1 pound fish
1 onion
salt
matzo meal

Grease pan with shortening. Dip fish into matzo meal (salt added). Cut onion and put in pan. Place fish on top. Bake in 350° oven for ½ hour.

Chuck Stew
Mother Satz
Favorite stew cooked on stove.

1 to 2 pounds chuck
1 chopped onion
1 garlic, chopped
2 sliced carrots
2 sliced celery
2 to 4 quartered potatoes
salt and pepper
dill and parsley

Place onion and garlic in Dutch oven. Add chuck cut into large pieces and place on top. Use low flame. Stir frequently and turn over meat occasionally. Cook around 15 minutes. Add 1 cup boiling water and cook for 1 hour or longer until almost tender. Add carrots and celery at that time and potatoes a little later. Add seasonings. More water can be added at any time. If desired, can thicken gravy with 1 or 2 tablespoons cornstarch mixed in 1 or 2 tablespoons cold water. Cook until meat and vegetables are done.

Brown Sugar Cookies
Mother Satz

½ cup vegetable shortening
2 eggs
2 teaspoons baking powder
½ cup Mazola oil
1 teaspoon salt
rind & juice of 1 orange
1 cup brown sugar

2½ cups flour
1 teaspoon vanilla
¾ cup nuts

Cream shortening and brown sugar. Add oil and mix well. Add eggs and beat well. Add orange juice and rind. Sift flour and baking powder and salt and add to other mixture. Beat well and add vanilla and nuts. Bake at 350° oven until light brown, about 10–15 minutes. Watch.

Brown Sugar Cookies #2
Mother Satz

½ cup brown sugar pressed down
¼ cup vegetable shortening
¼ cup Mazola oil
1 egg
1 orange juice and rind (squeezed, not strained)
1 cup flour

Cream sugar and shortening, then add oil and egg. Add flour and then orange juice and rind. Beat real well until spongy. If too loose, add 1 tablespoon flour. Bake in 350° oven for 8–10 minutes or longer.

Carrot Cookies
Mother Satz

1 cup sugar
2½ cups flour
2 eggs
½ cup vegetable shortening
½ cup Mazola oil

1 teaspoon salt
1 teaspoon baking powder
1 teaspoon vanilla
½ cup nuts, crushed
1 cup grated carrots

Mix all ingredients real well. Roll out and cut. Use 350° oven for around 15 minutes.

Apple Pie Crust
Mother Satz

1 egg
¼ cup Mazola oil
¼ cup shortening
½ cup sugar
1 teaspoon baking powder
½ teaspoon salt
2 cups flour
1 teaspoon vanilla
¼ cup cold water

Sift flour and make a ring. In center put in egg, shortening, oil, sugar, baking powder, salt, and vanilla. If too hard, add water. Divide into 2 rolls. Grease pan well. Roll out bottom crust first.

Apple Pie Filling
Mother Satz

sliced apples (4 to 6)
¼ cup sugar
1 teaspoon cinnamon

Mix sugar and cinnamon together. Fill pan with apples, sprinkle with sugar and cinnamon. Top with second crust and sprinkle again with sugar and cinnamon. Make air holes on top. Bake in 350° oven for 30 minutes or longer.

Apple Strudel
Mother Satz

Make above dough and place in refrigerator. After 1 hour take out and roll a little and warm up. Roll dough. Use Wesson oil from can. Mix cinnamon and sugar (make sugar dark). Sprinkle on dough. Grate apples. Squeeze out water. Put jam, then apples on dough. Roll up and cut into small rolls. Bake in 350° oven for 30 minutes or longer.

Recipes from Satz Family

Veal Chops
Fannie Goldman

Dry chops. Dip each side in beaten egg. Then dip mixture of flour and bread crumbs, seasoned with salt, pepper, (add paprika, if desired). Put in refrigerator for 1 hour. Brown each side in frying pan. Brown a diced onion at the same time. (Use a little grease in the frying pan—shortening or chicken fat). When chops and onion are lightly browned, placed in covered pan or roaster, add a little boiled water (don't pour the water over the meat, but rather on the side) and bake for one hour, in moderate oven, 350°.

Fabulous Fish
Fan Goldman

1 cup mayonnaise or miracle whip
⅓ cup sour cream
juice of ½ lemon
salt and pepper
a few drops of Tabasco sauce
(a few drops of tarragon if you have it on hand)
¼ cup or more of chopped parsley
¼ cup chopped onions
1 pound of fish fillets

Mix all ingredients (this can be done ahead). Line pan with foil and lay down fish fillets. Spread sauce to cover and bake about ½ hour or until sauce bubbles and is light brown at 350° oven.

Noodle Pudding
Fan Goldman

16-ounce package medium wide noodles
6 eggs beaten
salt
¾ cup sugar
1 carton (16-ounce) cottage cheese
1 carton (16-ounce) sour cream
1 stick melted butter

Beat eggs, add sugar. Add cooked and drained noodles. Add cottage cheese and sour cream. Melt the butter in 9 x 13 pan (or one a little longer if you have it and add most of the melted butter to above). Bake at 350° oven for 1 hour. You may swirl a jar (small) of apricot jam through mixture and top with cornflake crumbs rolled fine to which a little cinnamon and sugar has been added.

Date Bars
Fan Goldman

Filling:
½ teaspoon salt
3 cups dates cut up (1½ pounds)
¾ cup sugar
1 cup hot water
juice and rind of 1 lemon

Bring to a boil all of the above—stir and watch carefully—until thick—set aside.

Crust:
1¾ cup oatmeal
1½ cups flour
1 cup brown sugar
1 cup chopped nuts (or roll until pretty fine with rolling pin)
½ cup melted butter or margarine
1 teaspoon soda
2 heaping tablespoons sour cream
¾ teaspoon salt

Mix all ingredients thoroughly. Pat ½ of this mixture in a 9 x 13 greased pan. Add cooked dates. Add rest of crumb mixture on top. Bake for 25 minutes at 350° oven—only until light brown.

Cheese Blintzes
Fan Goldman
The batter should come out thin if you don't pour too much in your pan when frying it.

2 eggs, well beaten
1 cup flour
1 teaspoon salt
1½ cup water

Add water to well-beaten eggs, then add flour and salt gradually and stir until smooth.

Melt 1 teaspoon butter or margarine in a 7" skillet. Pour 1 tablespoon of the batter into it, turning the pan quickly so batter will cover the bottom. Fry until lightly browned on one side only. Stack the blintzes, browned side up on a towel until all the batter is used, adding additional butter or margarine as required.

Cheese Filling:
1½ pounds dry cottage cheese
1 or 2 egg yolks, beaten
1 tablespoon melted butter
salt, sugar, and cinnamon to taste

Mix cheese with egg yolks and butter and with salt, sugar, and cinnamon to taste. Place a tablespoon of mixture in center of each blintz. Fold edges over to form envelope. Fry in butter or margarine until brown on all sides, or bake in a moderate oven. Serve hot with sour cream, or with sugar and cinnamon mixture. *Freezes well.*

Chocolate Chip Bars
Fan Goldman

⅓ cup shortening or margarine (melted)
2 cups rolled quick oats
⅓ cup brown sugar (packed firmly)
¼ cup dark brown syrup (Karo)
½ teaspoon salt
1½ teaspoons vanilla
1 cup chocolate chips
¼ cup chopped nuts

Pour melted margarine over the rolled quick oats and mix well. Add the rest of the ingredients and stir until mixed well. Press into a 7" by 11" pan and bake about 25 minutes at 350°. (Don't over bake. Mixture will be bubbly but will harden as it cools.) Let cool slightly—cut into bars and finish cooling on wire rack. *Yum.*

Salmon Loaf
Fan Goldman

1 large can salmon
2 stalks celery, chopped
1 can mushroom soup
1 cup bread crumbs, or more
1 onion, chopped
3 eggs, beaten
1 tablespoon lemon juice
2 tablespoons mayonnaise

Sauté onions and celery. De-bone and skin salmon, and add onions and celery. Add eggs and rest of ingredients. Pour into ungreased loaf pan. Dot with butter or margarine. Bake 1 hour at 350°. It is even better with a cream cheese sauce with peas poured over.
Delicious!

French Dressing
Fan Goldman

¾ cup Wesson oil
¼ teaspoon paprika
¼ cup vinegar (plain or salad)
⅓ cup catsup
⅓ medium size grated onion
juice of ½ lemon
¼ cup sugar or less
½ teaspoon salt

Mix dry ingredients and add rest of ingredients and blend well.

Pecan Balls
Fan Goldman

½ pound butter or shortening
⅔ cups powdered sugar
Mix well. Add:
1 teaspoon cream (sweet)
1½ teaspoons vanilla
2 cups cake flour
1 cup broken nuts (walnuts or pecans)

Chill dough. (Put in refrigerator for ½ hour or longer, if convenient). Form small balls. Bake in 350° oven till light brown, 15–20 minutes. Roll in powdered sugar.

Perfect Beet Borscht (Meatless)
Dinah Elkin

9 medium-size beets, peeled and grated
1 whole medium onion
4 quarts cold water
juice from 2½ lemons
2 tablespoons salt
1 scant cup of sugar

Peel and grate beets into 4 quart pan. Add cold water about ½ inch from rim of pan. Cook uncovered until water comes to a boil. Add 2 tablespoons salt and 1 onion. When beets are tender, add juice from 2½ lemons and a scant cup of sugar. Cover and simmer another ½ hour. Discard onion. Cool and refrigerate in jars.

Suggestion:
Can parboil whole beets. Then peel and shred in food processor. Saves time and is much easier on the hands. Then follow rest of recipe above.

Beet Borscht (Dairy)
Dinah Elkin

Follow above recipe. When done, remove from flame. Pour into large bowl in which 3 eggs have been beaten and ½ pint of sweet cream added. Pour back and forth from bowl to pan until well mixed. Cool well before refrigerating. Store in jars for convenience.

Zucchini Casserole
Dinah Elkin

1 cup flour
1½ teaspoons shortening
½ teaspoon baking powder
¼ teaspoon soda
½ cup chopped onions
½ cup parmesan cheese
¼ teaspoon pepper
½ teaspoon oregano
1 teaspoon garlic powder
½ to 1 teaspoon dill
3 cups zucchini grated, unpeeled
½ cup oil
4 eggs
½ teaspoon salt

Mix the above ingredients together. Bake in a 9 x 13 pan in a 350° oven for about 25 minutes.

Baked Fryers
Dinah Elkin

6-7½ pounds fryers (use 9 x 13 or 10½ x 15 pan)

Lay out cut-up fryers so that all parts are touching. Fill in empty spaces with giblets.

Sprinkle with seasoned salt (Lawrey's), sprinkle garlic powder over top. Sprinkle paprika and sweet basil. Bake in 350° oven about 2 hours. Baste once or twice during baking. Place aluminum foil on bottom. Don't cover or cover loosely last ½ hour of baking.
Very tender and juicy.

Tuna Hot Dish
Dinah Elkin

2 cups raw Creamettes
2 cans (6-ounce) tuna, drained
2 cans mushroom soup
2 cups milk
season with black pepper and dill seed
1 cup shredded cheddar cheese
1 onion, diced
½ green pepper, diced
2-ounce jar pimento, drained

Mix all together in large bowl. Put in greased 9 x 12 pan, cover with foil. Do this the night before. Bake the next day in 350° oven about 45 minutes. Before baking may have to add a little milk. Check while baking to see if it needs more milk, as it should be nice and moist.
Serves 6–8

Adath Noodle Pudding
Dinah Elkin

1 pound noodles
1 quart buttermilk
4 eggs
½ cup sugar (or less)
¼ teaspoon salt
⅛ (2 tablespoons) butter or margarine

Cook noodles in salted water till tender; drain well. Beat eggs until fluffy. Melt margarine and add to noodles. Add sugar, eggs, salt, and buttermilk. Mix well. Turn into buttered 9 x 13 greased pan. Cover and bake 45 minutes at 350°.

Topping:
½ cup brown sugar
2 tablespoons melted margarine
½ cup cornflake crumbs
¼ teaspoon cinnamon

Mix all ingredients and sprinkle on top of kugel. Cover and bake 30 minutes or more. Let set 5–10 minutes before cutting.
Have cut before re-heating.
Great for covered dish.

Garlic Pasta Salad
Dinah Elkin

1 fancy pasta (rotini, etc.)
1 cup chopped onion
1 cup fine chopped green onions
1 cup chopped green pepper
1 cup chopped fresh tomatoes
1 cup chopped celery
1 cup fresh broccoli flowerettes
1 cup chopped water chestnuts

Dressing:
1 (5- or 6-ounce) bottle Creamy Italian Dressing
½–1 teaspoon garlic powder
salt and pepper

Cook pasta according to package directions. Mix all ingredients. Refrigerate 6–8 hours. Add tomatoes before serving. Garnish with hard-cooked eggs.

Pear Cake
Dinah Elkin

1½ cups vegetable oil
3 eggs
¾ teaspoon salt
1 teaspoon cinnamon
2 cups chopped canned pears (well drained)
1 cup chopped pecans (I use walnuts)
2 cups sugar (or less)
3 cups sifted flour
1 teaspoon baking soda
1 teaspoon vanilla

Grease and flour 10" Bundt pan. Spoon in batter, which will be thick.

Beat oil, sugar, and eggs together. Sift dry ingredients together and add to egg mixture. Add vanilla. Fold in chopped pears and nuts.

Bake in moderate slow oven 325° for 1 hour 20 minutes, or until cake tests done. Cool cake in pan 20 minutes, remove from pan and cool completely on cake rack. Optional: when cool, sprinkle with powdered sugar or frost with thin confectioners' sugar glaze, which can be made with syrup from canned pears.
Max's favorite

Meat Loaf
Dinah Elkin

1½ pounds ground beef
½–⅔ cups ketchup with water to equal 1 cup
¾ cup oats, uncooked
1 egg, beaten
¼ cup chopped onions
1 teaspoon salt
¼ teaspoon pepper
sweet basil
½ potato, grated (optional)
½ carrot, grated (optional)

"Chop" all ingredients together until well mixed. Shape in loaf pan and bake uncovered in 350° oven about 1 hour. If using 2 pounds meat, make 2 loaves.

Honey Poppy Seed Dressing
Dinah Elkin

⅔ cup honey
1⅓ cups peanut oil
2 tablespoons vinegar (white)
2 tablespoons Tachina
½ teaspoon salt
2 teaspoons poppy seeds
1 teaspoon dry mustard
2 tablespoons minced onions
3 tablespoons lemon juice
½ teaspoon (little more) garlic powder
Put all ingredients in jar and shake well to blend. Refrigerate.

Honey Cake
Dinah Elkin

1¼ cups white sugar
1 cup honey
¾ cup oil
1 cup hot coffee
1 teaspoon soda (mix coffee and soda together)
1 cup ground nuts
3 eggs
3 cups bread flour plus ¼ to ⅓ more
3 teaspoons baking powder
1 teaspoon allspice, optional (I prefer ½ teaspoon nutmeg)
¾ teaspoon salt
rind of orange plus 3 tablespoons Brandy

Beat eggs with sugar until light and thick. Add oil and then honey. Beat until well mixed. Sift dry ingredients together and add alternately with hot coffee. Add nuts and brandy last. Bake in 350° oven over an hour. Check.

Zucchini-Pineapple Bread
Dinah Elkin

3 eggs
1 cup oil (beat eggs and oil until thick and
   foamy)
2 teaspoons vanilla
2 cups shredded zucchini
1 cup well-drained pineapple (crushed and sugar
   free)
3 cups flour plus 2 tablespoons
1 teaspoon salt
3 teaspoons soda
½ teaspoon baking powder
1½ teaspoons cinnamon
½ teaspoon nutmeg
2 cups (scant) sugar
1 cup raisins

Add dry ingredients and zucchini mixture
alternately to egg mixture. Stir in both 1 cup nuts
and 1 cup raisins. Pour into 2 greased 8" loaf pans.
[I use 1 long (12") and 1 short (8").] Bake in 350°
oven 1 hour or longer.

Rocky Road Bars
Dinah Elkin

¼ cup flour
¼ teaspoon baking powder
⅛ salt

Sift together flour, baking powder, salt.
½ cup brown sugar, packed
1 egg
1 tablespoon softened butter or margarine

Mix together and beat together brown sugar, egg,
butter.

½ teaspoon vanilla
1 cup chopped walnuts
1 cup quartered marshmallows
1 6-ounce package chocolate chips

Grease 9" pan. Mix all ingredients together and
place marshmallows on top. Bake in 350° oven for
15–20 minutes until lightly brown and springs
back. Remove.
Delicious!

Eggplant Parmigiana
Joan Satz

1 large eggplant
¼ cup flour
1 egg, beaten slightly
2 tablespoons water
¾ cup dried bread crumbs
¾ tablespoon olive oil
½ teaspoon oregano
½ cup parmesan cheese
tomato sauce
½ teaspoon salt
½ pound mozzarella & Swiss cheese slices

Slice eggplant ½ inch thick—peel—dredge with
flour. Mix egg, water, and salt. Dip eggplant in
flour, then in egg mixture, then bread crumbs.
Refrigerate 30 minutes or longer to set coating.
Heat oil in skillet until hot. Cook slices slowly
until tender, both sides. Arrange in single layer in
greased pan. Distribute cheese slices over top.
Add tomato sauce over each slice. Sprinkle with
oregano and parmesan. Bake until cheese melts.
May be made ahead of time and refrigerated.
Bake in 400° oven for 10 minutes. *Serves 6.*
Great for people who love eggplant.

Pecan Pie
Joan Satz

⅓ **cup melted butter**
⅔ **cup sugar**
1 cup dark corn syrup
¼ **teaspoon salt**
3 eggs
1¼ cup pecans
1 9-inch unbaked pie shell

Beat together sugar, syrup, eggs, salt and add the melted butter and pecans. Pour into pie shell. Bake 50 minutes in 350° oven or until set. Serve warm.
Serves 8

Recipes from
Miriam Lerner Satz

Garden Fresh Herb Chicken

Miriam Satz

Favorite chicken recipe.

1 chicken cut into 8ths
1 medium size onion
6 stalks of chopped fresh chive
1 fresh dill seed head and leaves
1 minced garlic
few sprigs of fresh parsley

Wash chicken and place in baking pan. Heat oven to 325°. Cut onion, garlic, parsley, chives, and dill into small pieces. Mix together in dish. Spread over top of chicken. Sprinkle flour over all and add salt, pepper, and paprika to taste. Place a small amount of warm water in the bottom of the pan. Bake in oven for 1½ to 2 hours or until tender. (Potatoes may be baked in the oven at the same time.) Instead of flour can use matzo meal, cracker crumbs, or bread crumbs.

Baked Chicken with Corn Flake Crumbs

Miriam Satz

Cut large onion and 1 clove garlic and put in roasting pan. Season with salt, pepper, and paprika. Dip chicken in corn flake crumbs and place on onions. Add small amount of warm water in the bottom of the pan. Bake until golden brown, using 325° oven.

Four-Way Chicken (Israeli Style)
Miriam Satz

1 chicken, cut up
4 tablespoons honey
4 tablespoons lemon juice
4 tablespoons margarine
4 tablespoons soy sauce

Place chicken in baking dish, skin side down. Combine remaining ingredients in a saucepan and cook over low heat until dissolved. Pour over chicken. Bake uncovered at 350° for 1 hour, turning once and basting frequently until covered with a rich brown sauce.

Everybody's Favorite Chicken
Miriam Satz

1 bottle Wish-Bone Russian dressing
1 cup boiling water
1 package dehydrated onion soup
2 onions, sliced
5–6 pieces of chicken
3 tablespoons apricot preserves
2 potatoes, sliced

Combine soup and water. Add Russian dressing and preserves. Mix well. Let set for about 2 hours.

Line bottom of Pyrex dish with layer of onions, then layer of potatoes, then chicken; pour sauce over all. Bake at 325° oven for 1½ hours. Baste every 20 minutes.

Easy Crispy Chicken
Miriam Satz

1 chicken (2½ to 3 pounds), cut up
about ½ stick or more margarine (parve), melted
about 2 cups of crispy rice cereal, slightly crushed

Rinse chicken pieces; pat dry with paper towels. Dip chicken pieces in melted margarine, then in cereal to coat. Place chicken pieces on a foil-lined baking sheet (the foil is easy for clean-up). Bake in a preheated 350° oven 45 to 60 minutes, or until chicken is tender and golden brown.

Chinese Chicken Breast with Vegetables
Miriam Satz

2 cups chicken breast (boneless)
1 cup carrots
4 tablespoons cooking oil (peanut)
1 tablespoon cornstarch
1 cup green pepper
1 teaspoon salt
2 tablespoons soy sauce

Cut chicken breast, green pepper, and carrots into pieces. Put chicken breast in a mixing bowl, add salt, cornstarch, soy sauce, and 1 tablespoon oil, mix well. With medium heat, pour 2 tablespoons oil in frying pan (or wok). When the oil is hot, add chicken. Fry and stir for 5 minutes and take from pan. Pour 1 tablespoon oil in pan, when hot, add carrots and stir, then add green pepper and stir for a few minutes. Add the chicken and mix well.

Cook vegetables to your preference. Celery, broccoli, and onion can be used instead of the above vegetables.
Serves 8

Chuck Roast
Miriam Satz

Cut 1 large onion and 1 clove garlic and place in a roasting pan. Lay chuck roast (3 to 4 pounds) over it; season with salt and pepper. Add fresh dill and parsley. Add small amount of warm water. Bake for ½ hour, uncovered in a 325° oven. Then add 2 tablespoons ketchup or Manischewitz tomato and mushroom sauce poured over the top of the roast. Add sliced carrots and celery at this time. Also, add more water, about 1 to 2 cups. Cover pan and cook for several hours until almost done. Then add quartered potatoes and cook uncovered. May add more water if needed. Can use 1 tablespoon cornstarch mixed with a little cold water for thickening, if desired.

Rolled Roast
Miriam Satz

Slice 1 onion and 1 clove garlic and place in roasting pan. Lay 3 to 4 pounds rolled roast over the onions. Use a meat thermometer. Add a little warm water. Bake uncovered in a 325° oven for several hours. Can add carrots, celery, potatoes, dill, and parsley to pan when the meat is almost done. Add more water and thicken with cornstarch, if desired.

London Broil
Miriam Satz

1 tablespoon margarine
¼ teaspoon salt
2 medium onions, thinly sliced

Melt margarine in skillet. Add onions and ¼ teaspoon salt; cook and stir until onions are tender. Keep warm over low heat.

2 tablespoons salad oil
1 teaspoon lemon juice
2 pounds flank steak
2 cloves garlic, crushed
1/2 teaspoon salt
1/2 teaspoon pepper

Stir together salad oil, lemon juice, garlic, ½ teaspoon salt, and the pepper; brush on top side of meat. Set oven control to broil and/or 550°. Broil 2 or 3 inches from heat about 5 minutes or until brown. Turn meat, brush with oil mixture and broil 5 minutes longer. Cut meat across grain at a slanted angle into thin slices; serve with onions. *Freezes well. 6–8 servings*

London Broil in a Wok
Miriam Satz

Follow above directions for broiling the meat. Slice thin as much as needed and marinate in a sauce.

Chinese Sauce for Vegetables
Miriam Satz

Blend until smooth 1 tablespoon cornstarch and 3 tablespoons cold water. Add ½ teaspoon salt and 1 tablespoon soy sauce.

Slice London Broil thin and cover with sauce. Cover and place in refrigerator for several hours. Mix occasionally.

When close to dinner hour, place 1 or 2 cloves of garlic cut in half in wok or skillet. Add 2 tablespoons peanut oil. Cook on high heat until garlic is brown. Discard. Take meat out of marinate and place in wok. Cook and turn occasionally, about 5 minutes, until red color disappears. Take out meat and set aside.

Cut up different vegetables—carrots, zucchini, broccoli, celery, onions, cabbage, green pepper, and add to wok. May need more peanut oil. Cook until vegetables are crisp but tender. Add sauce to vegetables and then meat. Mix well together. Serve with cooked rice.

Brisket
Miriam Satz

3 to 4 pounds beef brisket
2 sliced onions
2 cloves garlic, cut up

Place brisket on rack in roasting pan. Onions and garlic are put on top. Add pepper and a little water. Baste often. (Optional: Put a little mustard on top before the onions, if desired.) Cover roaster and use 350° oven for ½ to 1 hour and then turn oven down to 325° for 2 more hours or until meat is tender. Take gravy and pour over meat. Separate at first. May add sliced carrots, celery, and quartered potatoes toward end of cooking. Add fresh dill and parsley about the middle of the baking.

Fikonicas (Greek-Style Cholent)
Miriam Satz

2 cups small dry white beans
1 large onion, chopped
oil
½ pound cubed stewing meat
   (more can be used if desired)
boiling water
salt and pepper

Soak beans overnight. Brown onion slowly in a small amount of oil until dark brown but not burned. Add beans, meat, salt, and pepper and enough boiling water to more than cover. Cook slowly for at least three hours, but five would be better.

Kasha
Miriam Satz

Can be used in soups, with meat gravy and mixed with cooked shell macaroni or bow-ties.

1 cup kasha
1 egg
1 teaspoon salt
2 tablespoons olive oil
2 cups boiling water

Mix 1 cup kasha with 1 egg, add salt. Heat 2 tablespoons olive oil in skillet. Add kasha and cook uncovered until the kasha crisps, about 5 minutes. Add 2 cups boiling water, turn heat down, and cover and cook about 15 minutes or until the kasha is tender and liquid is absorbed.

New York Frankfurters
Miriam Satz

Slice 1 onion, garlic and sauté in olive oil. Add red pepper flakes, paprika, and 1 cup Madeira sauce. Mix and stir over heat. Cook frankfurters in boiling water about 10 minutes. Place meat in buns and put onion sauce on top.

Italian Spaghetti and Meat Balls
Miriam Satz
The best spaghetti sauce.

Meat Balls:
2 pounds ground beef
2 eggs
1 medium onion, chopped or grated
1 teaspoon salt (or a little soy sauce)

pepper, to taste
½ cup cold water
2 to 4 tablespoons cracker crumbs or bread crumbs

Mix all ingredients together thoroughly and form into balls. Fry in a little olive oil in Dutch oven or heavy skillet. Remove meat balls from skillet after they are browned.

Sauce:
1 large onion, chopped
2 tablespoons chopped parsley
1 stalk celery, chopped
1 clove garlic, minced
2 small cans tomato paste or 1 large can
1 small can tomato sauce or 1 large can
1 quart canned tomatoes
1 quart tomato juice
1 small can water
salt, pepper, sugar to taste
1 small can mushrooms (optional)
fresh dill
cooked spaghetti

Put small amount of olive oil in skillet. Add chopped onion, parsley, celery, garlic, and mushrooms. Cook until onion is transparent. Transfer this mixture to a Dutch oven or heavy pot and add the remaining ingredients. Cook around 2 hours. Add meat balls and cook 1 hour longer. Serve sauce and meatballs over cooked spaghetti. Do not mix sauce and spaghetti together ahead of time.
Serves 10 to 12

Russian Meat Balls
Miriam Satz

1 egg
1 teaspoon salt
¼ teaspoon pepper
3 tablespoons olive oil
3 tablespoons minced onion
1 pound ground beef
1 cup tomato juice
1 green pepper, diced
¼ cup diced celery

Add egg, salt, pepper, and 1½ teaspoons minced onion to meat. Mix well. Form into balls and brown in hot olive oil. Place balls in a baking dish with green pepper, celery, and remaining onion. Pour tomato juice over all. Cover and bake in moderate oven, 350°, 1 hour or longer.
Serves 6 to 8

Lazy Baked Chicken
Miriam Satz

6 large chicken thighs
salt
black pepper

Preheat oven to 400°. Lightly salt and pepper chicken on all sides and under skin. Bake uncovered 35 minutes in 8 x 8 baking dish. Shut off heat and let cook ½ hour longer.

Israeli Chicken
Miriam Satz
Madelyn Satz's favorite

8 chicken breasts (single) or legs
1 cup sliced mushrooms
⅓ cup soy sauce
1 teaspoon paprika, sugar, vinegar,
   and catsup
½ teaspoon garlic powder
water

Combine the soy sauce, paprika, vinegar, garlic powder, catsup, and enough water to make 1 cup. Add mushrooms. Place chicken breasts, skin side up, in pan and pour sauce and mushrooms over chicken. Cover with aluminum foil and bake at 350° oven for 30 minutes. Uncover and bake until brown (approximately 20 minutes longer.) Baste with sauce frequently once chicken is uncovered. Serve with rice. Can be used for Rose Hashanah or Sabbath.
Delicious!

Chicken Diable
Miriam Satz

1 fryer, cut up
4 tablespoons margarine, melted
½ cup honey
¼ cup prepared mustard
1 teaspoon salt
¼ teaspoon curry powder

Melt margarine in shallow pan; add all other ingredients except chicken. Roll chicken in this mixture and place meaty side up. Bake at 375° for 1 hour or until tender and glazed.

Chili Con Carne
Miriam Satz

1½ to 2 pounds ground beef
1 package pinto beans cooked
1 quart tomato juice
1 can tomato soup
cooked rice
½ package chili mix
1 can whole kernel corn
1 quart canned tomatoes
1 small can tomato paste

Soak pinto beans overnight. Drain. Add fresh water and cook until beans are tender. Use a small amount of olive oil in skillet to brown ground beef. Add chili mix and stir well. Cook for a few minutes. Transfer to a Dutch oven or large heavy pot and add rest of ingredients. Cook for several hours and stir often. When done, serve chili over cooked rice. *Freezes well.*

"Souper" Chicken
Miriam Satz

1 chicken, cut in 8 pieces
1 can tomato soup
¼ cup brown sugar
juice of ½ lemon

Preheat oven to 350°. Put chicken in a greased pan. Combine remaining ingredients and pour over chicken. Bake for 1½ hours, until chicken is browned and tender.

Sweet and Sour Stuffed Peppers
Miriam Satz

6 green peppers
1 pound ground beef
½ cup cooked rice or 1/2 cup dry bread crumbs
1 carrot, grated
½ teaspoon salt
⅛ teaspoon pepper
2 eggs
1 onion, grated

Combine all ingredients and mix well. Stuff prepared peppers. (Cut off stem ends of pepper. If very large, cut into half lengthwise, remove seeds and inner white ribs. Parboil by dropping into boiling water. Remove from fire and let stand in the water about 5 minutes. Drain well.) Place in casserole and add small amount of water. Cover and bake in moderate oven (350°) 40 minutes. Uncover. Add sweet and sour sauce. Increase heat to 400°. Bake 10 minutes longer.
Serves 6

Stuffed Cabbage Leaves and Cabbage Soup
Miriam Satz

1 head cabbage
1 pound ground beef
½ cup cooked rice
1 egg
1 teaspoon salt
⅛ teaspoon pepper

½ cup raisins (optional)
1 onion sliced thin
juice of 1 lemon
about ¼ cup brown sugar
2 cups canned tomatoes
1 cup water

Place cabbage in boiling water for 5 minutes to soften. Combine meat, rice, salt, and pepper. Put a generous amount on each leaf. Fold in sides. Roll up and fasten with toothpicks. Shred the heart of cabbage. Line a large pot with shredded cabbage. Put stuffed cabbage on top, close together. Add remaining cabbage, onion, raisins (optional), lemon juice, sugar, tomatoes, and water. Simmer gently 2½ to 3 hours. *Freezes well.*
Serves 6

Cabbage Soup:

Add more water, 1 quart tomato juice, 1 quart tomatoes, 1 can tomato soup to above recipe. Move pan back and forth occasionally. Cover pot. The above recipe can be doubled easily, except 1 head of cabbage should be enough. Freeze in quart containers.

Sweet and Sour Sauce
Miriam Satz

1 cup tomato sauce or puree
½ cup water
3 tablespoons lemon juice
3 tablespoons brown sugar
⅛ teaspoon paprika
½ cup raisins (optional)

Combine all ingredients in saucepan and cook over moderate heat 10 minutes. Pour sauce over stuffed green peppers and bake 10 minutes longer.

Stuffed Zucchini with Ground Beef
Miriam Satz

6–8 large zucchini
½ pound ground beef
2 tablespoons grated tomatoes
chopped parsley
fresh dill
1 large onion
½ cup cooked rice
1 tablespoon pine nuts (optional)
salt and pepper
flour

Peel and core the zucchini. Mix together the remaining ingredients, except for the flour, and use to stuff the zucchini. Roll in flour. Place in baking dish. Cover with water and sprinkle with salt and pepper. Bake at 350° until soft. Mix together a few tablespoons tomato paste, some more chopped parsley, and a tablespoon sugar. Add to the water in the baking dish and bake for 30 minutes more.

Beef and Eggplant (Greek Musaca)
Miriam Satz
For lovers of eggplant.

1 large eggplant
salt and pepper
olive oil
1 large onion, minced
1 pound ground beef
2 cups canned tomatoes

Peel the eggplant and cut into ½-inch thick slices. Sprinkle each slice with salt and let stand 1 hour. Drain and brown eggplant in hot olive oil. (Or spray PAM on cookie sheet, add eggplant and broil until brown on top and turn over once.) Sauté onions in olive oil until transparent. Add beef, seasoned with salt and pepper to taste. Cook together until slightly brown. Place alternate layers of meat mixture and eggplant in casserole. Pour tomatoes over this. Bake in slow oven (325°) 1 hour.
Serves 6

Ground Beef Macaroni Casserole
Miriam Satz

1 8-ounce package macaroni
½ pound ground beef
2 tablespoons olive oil
½ cup water
sliced mushrooms
1 can tomato soup
½ cup bread crumbs
6–8 black olives or stuffed olives

Cook macaroni according to directions. Brown ground beef in olive oil along with a couple of mushrooms, if you have them on hand. Slice up olives. Then stir water into the tomato soup. Add the meat and olives. Stir this sauce into the hot, drained macaroni and pour the whole business into a large greased baking dish or 4 individual dishes. Sprinkle with bread crumbs. If you like, add sliced mushrooms on top. Bake in 350° oven for 20 minutes or longer.

Chafing Dish Meatballs
Miriam Satz

2 pounds chopped meat
1 large onion, grated
1 egg, slightly beaten
salt to taste

Combine ingredients and shape into small balls.
Makes about 50 to 60

Sauce:
1 12-ounce bottle of chili sauce (or less)
1 10-ounce jar grape jelly (or less)
juice of 1 lemon

Mix ingredients and simmer. Drop in meatballs and simmer for about 45 minutes. Refrigerate and freeze until needed. Remove hardened fat. Reheat in chafing dish and serve with cocktail picks.
Delicious appetizer for company.

Lamb Pilaf
Miriam Satz

2 pounds lamb breast
2 large onions, sliced
salt and pepper
4 cups hot water
1½ cups raw rice

Brown meat and onions in olive oil in heavy pot. Season with salt and pepper. Continue braising until meat is very dark, stir very often, scraping bottom of pan. Add hot water, rice, salt, and pepper. Cover and bake in a slow oven (300°) 2 hours.

Variations:
Potatoes (as many as desired), 1 pound kidney beans soaked over night, or whole grain buckwheat (kasha) may be substituted for the rice.
Serves 6 to 8

Barbecued Lamb Breast (or Beef Short-Ribs)
Miriam Satz

2 pounds breast of lamb
1 teaspoon salt
pepper
½ cup chili sauce
¼ teaspoon red pepper
1 tablespoon vinegar
1 cup water
1 medium onion, sliced

Cut lamb into serving pieces. Season with salt and pepper. Place in hot skillet and brown fatty sides. Mix chili sauce, red pepper, vinegar, and water, pour over lamb. Add onion mixture. Cover. Simmer 1½ hours. Remove lid and cook on medium heat about 20 minutes, until barbecue sauce is almost absorbed.
Serves 4

Greek Lamb with String Beans
Miriam Satz

2 onions, minced
1 pound string beans, diced
1½ pounds lamb, cut in small pieces
salt and pepper to taste

Cover. Simmer until tender, about 30 minutes.
Serves 4

Stuffed Breast of Veal
Miriam Satz

Have butcher bone and cut pocket in breast. Fill evenly with favorite stuffing. Place on rack in open roasting pan. Roast in slow oven (300°) until well done, allowing 30 to 35 minutes per pound.

Stuffing for Veal Breast
Miriam Satz

½ onion, chopped
1 stalk celery, chopped
¾ to 1 cup flour
fresh parsley
2 eggs, beaten
2 tablespoons water
salt, pepper, paprika, garlic powder

Sauté onion and celery in olive oil until onion is transparent. Mix eggs with onion mixture, add chopped parsley, if desired. Add 2 tablespoons water and as much flour as needed to make a rather stiff dough. Season to taste. Stuff veal breast with the filling.

Veal Steak in Tomato Sauce
Miriam Satz

Cut 2 pounds of veal steak (½ inch thick) into 6 pieces. Dredge in flour seasoned with salt and pepper. Brown on both sides in hot fat (olive oil). Add 2 cups tomato juice. Cover. Simmer 1 hour.
Serves 6

Paprika Schnitzel
Miriam Satz

2 pounds veal steak
salt and pepper
flour
2 tablespoons fat (olive oil)
paprika
3 onions, sliced

Cut steak into serving pieces. Sprinkle with salt and pepper. Roll in flour. Melt fat in a skillet. Add enough paprika to make it red. Fry onions until transparent. Add meat. Fry until golden brown all over. Cover and cook slowly for ½ hour. Add a little water or stock if necessary.
Serves 6

Baked Veal, Russian Style
Miriam Satz

2 pounds veal cutlet
salt and pepper
wine vinegar
2 tablespoons olive oil
2 onions, sliced
3 tomatoes, sliced

Season veal with salt and pepper. Place in a deep bowl and add vinegar to cover. Marinate 1 hour.

Drain, dry, and place veal in greased casserole. Brown in hot oven (450°). Brown onion and tomato slices in oil. Add to veal. Reduce heat to 300° and add stock or water to just cover. Bake 30 to 45 minutes longer.
Serves 6

Creamed Sole or Haddock
Miriam Satz

Cut one onion in pieces and put in greased pan. Add fish. Dilute can of cream of celery or mushroom soup with ¼ can milk and ¼ can water. Add touch of curry seasoning. Mix and pour over fish. Add a little salt, pepper, and paprika, and dot with pieces of butter over top. Bake in 375° oven for 45 minutes. Serve with mashed potatoes.

Baked Fish
(Flounder, Sole, Haddock)
Miriam Satz

4 pieces of fish
1 medium sliced onion
2 tablespoons fresh chopped dill
2 tablespoons dry white wine or lemon juice
salt and pepper
1 medium sliced tomato
2 tablespoons margarine

Wash fish. Pat dry and sprinkle with a little salt and pepper. Lightly brown onion in a little margarine (or melt margarine in casserole in oven), place in casserole dish, covering the bottom with the browned onion. Place fish on top then a layer of sliced tomatoes. Sprinkle with dill and dot with remaining margarine. Bake at 400° for 15 minutes. Pour wine over fish and bake for ten minutes or until fish is done.
The fish turns over very flaky and is delicious.

Broiled Salmon Steak or Fillet
Miriam Satz

Spray broiling dish with PAM. Wash and dry 4 pieces of salmon steak or 1 large fillet. Place on broiling pan and sprinkle Wondra flour or regular flour lightly over fish. Dot with pieces of butter or margarine and sprinkle with lemon juice. Broil until light brown and turn over once.
Great for company.

Fried Fish
(Flounder, Haddock, Sole or Trout)
Miriam Satz

1 pound fish filets
½ cup corn meal
¼ cup flour
sliced onions, if desired
salt, pepper, and paprika to taste

Wash fish filets and dry with paper towel. Mix corn meal with flour and dip fish into mixture. Heat cooking oil (olive) in skillet and add fish. Sprinkle salt, pepper, and paprika to taste. Add onions, if desired. Cook until bottom of fish appears golden brown; turn over and cook until done. Remove fish and onions to platter and serve at once.

Broiled Trout or Whiting Fish
Miriam Satz

Wash and clean fish. Dry on paper towel. Dip in ½ cup cornmeal (sometimes add a little flour). Place in broiling pan that has been sprayed with PAM. Dot with small pieces of butter or margarine. Sprinkle lemon juice over the fish. Broil until brown and turn over once and continue to broil until brown. Add salt and pepper to taste.

Trout in Envelopes for Two
Miriam Satz

2 trout with heads
olive oil, melted butter, or margarine
salt and pepper to taste
juice of ¼ lemon
2 tablespoons white wine

Brush each trout outside with oil or melted butter or margarine. Season with salt and pepper; sprinkle with lemon juice. Lay each trout in center of well-buttered oblong piece of foil. Add 1 tablespoon wine to each package. Fold and seal ends of foil; place side by side on shallow baking pan. Do not turn packages during baking. Bake at 400° 25–30 minutes. Serve trout in envelopes.

Hot Tuna Bread
Miriam Satz

1 (6½- to 7-ounce) can tuna, drained and flaked
2 tablespoons chopped parsley
⅓ cup sour cream
2 tablespoons lemon juice
1 loaf French bread—15 inches
2 tablespoons margarine
⅓ cup mayonnaise
1 tablespoon chopped pimento
¼ teaspoon garlic salt
¼ pound sliced Swiss cheese

Combine tuna, parsley, mayonnaise, sour cream, pimento, lemon juice, and salt. Slice bread lengthwise, place on baking sheet. Top with cheese, then mixture. Bake in 350° oven 25 minutes or until lightly brown.
Great for brunch.

Tuna, Noodle, and Mushroom Soup Casserole
Miriam Satz
An excellent emergency dish.

Preheat oven to 450°. Have ready:
2 to 3 cups boiled noodles

Drain:
1 can tuna fish, 7-ounce

Separate it with a fork into large flakes.
Do not mince it. Grease an ovenproof dish.
Arrange a layer of noodles, then sprinkle it with
fish and so on, with noodles on top.

Pour over this mixture:
1 cup condensed mushroom soup

Season the soup with:
Worcestershire sauce, curry powder
   (tip of knife), or dry sherry
¼ cup chopped parsley

Cover the top with:
buttered cornflakes or cracker crumbs
Bake until the top is brown.

Summer Tomato Sauce
Miriam Satz

2 large, ripe tomatoes
4 tablespoons olive oil
¼ cup chopped fresh basil leaves
¼ cup chopped scallions
1 tablespoon chopped fresh oregano leaves (or 1
   teaspoon dried)
2 cloves minced garlic
freshly ground pepper and salt to taste
(optional) freshly grated Parmesan cheese
1 8-ounce package of cooked thin spaghetti

Plunge tomatoes in a saucepan of boiling water
and blanch 30 seconds. Plunge in cold water.
Drain and peel. Remove cores of tomatoes and
squeeze to remove seeds. Dice pulp.

Combine diced tomatoes with 1 tablespoon
olive oil in a bowl. Add all remaining ingredients
except Parmesan and toss to blend. Refrigerate
until ready to serve, at least several hours.

When ready to serve, have sauce at room
temperature. Add remaining 3 tablespoons olive
oil and toss with hot pasta.

Variation:
Sprinkle with grated cheese for a dairy dish.
Makes 2 cups
Great fresh garden dish.

Easy Cottage Cheese and Noodle Dish
Miriam Satz
Martin's favorite noodle dish.

1 12-ounce package of broad or extra-broad
  noodles
1 egg (no yolks)
1 carton cottage cheese
salt, pepper, paprika to taste
1 tablespoon olive oil

Cook noodles according to directions. Drain. Add 1 beaten egg, cottage cheese and season with salt, pepper, and paprika. Heat olive oil in large skillet. Add noodle mixture and cook until bottom crisps. Stir and turn over and crisp mixture again. It may take 20 to 30 minutes to complete.

Broccoli and Zucchini Soup
Miriam Satz

1½ pounds beef cubes
1 marrow bone
cut up vegetables such as carrots, celery, onion,
  cabbage as desired
1 can whole kernel corn
broccoli and zucchini
noodles
season with salt and pepper
sprig of parsley
sprig of dill

Place beef cubes and marrow bone in large pot. Add cut-up vegetables and whole kernel corn. Fill pot with water almost to the top. Cook uncovered until water comes to a boil. Spoon off the scum that forms on the top.

Cover soup and turn down the flame. When beef is almost done, add the cut broccoli and sliced zucchini and noodles to the soup. Season with salt and pepper. Any type of noodle can be added last—such as alphabets, broad noodles, or macaroni.

Variation:
Make Mother Satz's egg dumplings and drop small amounts from a teaspoon into soup and cook until done.

Zucchini Vegetable Soup
Miriam Satz

1½ beef cubes
1 marrow bone
cut up vegetables such as carrots, celery, onion,
  cabbage
green or yellow fresh beans
peas
¼ cup quick barley
1 can tomato soup
1 peeled and cubed large potato
season with salt and pepper

Place beef cubes and marrow bone in large soup pot. Add vegetables, barley, tomato soup. Cook uncovered until water comes to a boil. Skim off the scum that has formed on top. Season with salt and pepper. After water has boiled and beef is tender, about 2 to 2½ hours later, add sliced zucchini and potato. Mother Satz's egg dumplings can be added. Cover pot and cook until done.

Right-Away Monterey Pasta
Miriam Satz

8-ounce package elbow macaroni (2 cups)
3 tablespoons butter or margarine
3 tablespoons flour
3 cups milk
12-ounce Monterey Jack cheese, grated medium-
  fine
paprika

Cook the macaroni according to package directions using the time suggested for pasta that is to be used in a cooked dish. Drain in a colander; cover.

In a 2-quart saucepan, over low heat, melt the butter or margarine. Stir in the flour. Off heat,

gradually stir in the milk, keeping smooth. Cover over moderately low heat, stirring constantly, until thickened and boiling.

Spread half the cooked macaroni (about 2 cups) over the bottom of a buttered shallow 2-quart baking dish (11¾ by 7½ by 1¼ inches). Sprinkle with half the cheese. Layer with the remaining macaroni. Sprinkle with the remaining cheese. Pour the still hot sauce as evenly as possible over the top. Sprinkle with the paprika.

Bake uncovered in a preheated 400° oven until bubbling around the edges and hot in the center (test with a fork—about 20 minutes). Let stand 5 minutes or so before serving. The cheese will be pully and chewy.
Makes 6 servings
Delicious dairy meal.

Corn and Lima Bean Chowder (Dairy)
Miriam Satz

1 cup dried lima beans
2 cups water
1 teaspoon salt
2 tablespoons chopped onion
¼ cup cooking fat (olive oil)
1 cup diced celery
1½ cups whole kernel corn
2 teaspoons salt
1 teaspoon sugar
⅛ teaspoon pepper
½ cup water
3 cups milk

Soak beans in 2 cups water several hours. Add salt. Cook until tender. This should make 2 cups cooked beans. Lightly brown onion in hot fat; add celery, corn, salt, sugar, pepper, and water. Simmer ½ hour. Add 2 cups cooked dried lima beans and the milk. Heat thoroughly.

Variations:

Can substitute navy beans or broccoli for the limas. The soup becomes non-dairy if no milk is used.

Serves 6

Sunshine Salad
Miriam Satz
Attractive dish for dinner.

1 cup boiling water
½ cup cold water
⅛ teaspoon salt
1 can (8¾-ounces) crushed pineapple
½ cup shredded carrots
1 package (3-ounces) orange or lemon flavored gelatin

Pour boiling water over gelatin in bowl, stirring until gelatin is dissolved. Stir in cold water, salt, and pineapple (with syrup). Chill until slightly thickened but not set. Stir in carrots. Pour into 4-cup ring mold or into 6 individual molds. Chill until firm.

Serves 6

Cabbage Salad
Miriam Satz

2 cups shredded cabbage
½ cup thinly sliced celery
2 radishes, chopped
small piece of diced Kosher dill
½ teaspoon salt
1½ tablespoons mayonnaise
½ cup shredded carrots
¼ cup chopped green pepper
¼ cup chopped onion
1 teaspoon sugar
1 teaspoon cider vinegar

Combine cabbage, carrots, celery, green pepper, onion, radish, pickle, salt, sugar, and vinegar. Moisten with mayonnaise. Mix lightly. Arrange on crisp lettuce. Sprinkle with minced parsley or paprika. May be garnished with orange slices.

Serves 6

Sweet Potatoes Candied with Brown Sugar
Miriam Satz

Combine and bring to boil ¾ cup brown sugar, ⅓ cup water, ½ teaspoon salt, and 2 tablespoons butter or margarine. Place halves of 6 cooked medium-size sweet potatoes in greased baking dish and pour over mixture. Bake in moderate oven (350°) 15 to 20 minutes, basting frequently with syrup.

Serves 6

French Dressing
Miriam Satz
Great for salads.

1 8-ounce can tomato sauce
½ cup sugar
½ cup oil
¼ cup vinegar
½ teaspoon Worcestershire sauce
½ teaspoon celery seed
½ teaspoon dry mustard
½ teaspoon paprika
½ teaspoon garlic salt
½ teaspoon salt
½ teaspoon pepper

Place all ingredients in a deep bowl and mix with rotary beater. Makes 1 pint. Keeps indefinitely in the refrigerator.

Stewed String Beans
Miriam Satz

2 tablespoons peanut oil
2 scallions, shredded
1 teaspoon shredded ginger if available
1 tablespoon soy sauce
1 cup water
¾ pound string beans cut in 1" lengths
salt to taste

In the wok or skillet heat peanut oil. Stir scallions and ginger in the oil. Add soy sauce and water and bring to a boil. Add beans and mix well. Cover and simmer over low heat until liquid is reduced and beans are tender, about 20 minutes. Serve hot.

Easy Macaroni Salad
Miriam Satz

1 cup uncooked shell macaroni
1 tablespoon vinegar
1 clove garlic, minced
½ cup celery, chopped
1 carrot, grated
1 tablespoon oil
¼ cup onion, finely chopped
1 teaspoon salt
¼ cup chopped dill pickle
⅓ cup mayonnaise

Cook macaroni according to package directions. Drain. While macaroni is still hot sprinkle with oil (olive) and vinegar. Combine macaroni with rest of ingredients and chill.
Serves 4-6
Good for covered dish and picnics.

Butternut Squash
Miriam Satz

**1 squash, cut into small chunks (peel squash with
  potato peeler)**
½ cup chopped green pepper
½ cup chopped celery
½ cup cooked rice
**salt, pepper, garlic powder, or leave out and use
  soy sauce for seasoning**
2 tablespoons olive oil
½ onion, chopped
chopped chives, parsley, and dill (optional)
2 cut up tomatoes

Put 2 tablespoons olive oil in skillet. Heat oil and
add the vegetables, seasoning, then the rice and top
with the cut tomatoes. Place cover on skillet, turn
heat down low and simmer until done—perhaps
15 to 20 minutes.

Variation:
Can substitute zucchini for the butternut.
Great for covered dish and picnics.

Oil Free Eggplant
Miriam Satz

Peel. Slice eggplant ½ inch thick. Season
(with perhaps pepper and oregano). Roll in
cornmeal, flour, or bread crumbs. Place on a
cookie sheet sprayed with PAM, bake at
350° about 15 minutes on each side.

Scalloped Tomatoes
Miriam Satz

3 cups tomatoes (canned or fresh)
1 medium cucumber, pared and sliced
salt
1 small onion, sliced
½ cup bread crumbs, buttered
½ cup grated cheese
pepper

Into a greased baking dish or casserole, place a
layer of tomatoes, add half the cucumber and
onion slices and half of the crumbs. Repeat with
more tomatoes and remaining cucumbers, onions,
and crumbs. Top with tomatoes and sprinkle with
cheese. Bake in moderate oven (375°) 40 minutes.

Broccoli Casserole
Miriam Satz
Stephanie's favorite.

2 packages frozen chopped broccoli
1 can water chestnuts, chopped
½ stick butter or margarine
½ cup pecans, chopped
1 package onion soup mix
bread crumbs

Cook broccoli until just tender, not mushy. Drain.
Melt butter or margarine and soup mix to soften.
Mix all together and pour into casserole; top with
bread crumbs. Bake in moderate oven (350°) until
browned or thoroughly heated (does not take
long).

Stuffed Mushrooms
Miriam Satz
Great appetizer.

1 pound fresh mushrooms. Clean and separate caps from stems. Cut the stems into little pieces. Dice 1 onion and sauté both in margarine. Add approximately ½ cup to 1 cup matzo meal or bread crumbs. Season with salt and pepper or use soy sauce. Add a little cooking wine. Add egg and stir mixture. Place small amount of mixture on caps and bake on a greased sheet using a 350° oven for 20 minutes.
Delicious!

Walnut Snack
Miriam Satz
Good with any drink.

Spread 1 cup walnut halves in shallow pan. Dot with butter. Heat 350°—15 minutes. Stir occasionally. Remove from oven. Sprinkle liberally with onion salt. Cool on paper towels.

Cucumber Salad
Miriam Satz
Best when cucumbers are from garden.

2 large cucumbers
½ cup white vinegar
2 tablespoons water
¼ cup sugar
½ teaspoon salt
few grinds of black pepper
2 tablespoons chopped parsley

Do not peel the cucumbers unless they are heavily waxed. Score them with the tines of a fork before slicing very thin. In a deep bowl, combine the remaining ingredients and mix well. Add the cucumber slices; cover them with a plate and a weight. Refrigerate about 3 hours. Drain the cucumbers to serve. The marinade can be saved and used again.

Variations:
Add a thinly sliced onion to the above recipe. Sprinkle the insides of scooped out tomatoes with salt and pepper; fill with Cucumber salad, bathed in lowfat yogurt.
Serves 4

Sliced Cucumber Pickles
Miriam Satz

12 medium size cucumbers
2 onions
½ cup salt
4 quarts water
2 cups cider vinegar
1 cup sugar
1½ teaspoon turmeric
1 teaspoon celery seed
1 teaspoon mustard seed

Wash, clean, and slice cucumbers. Peel and slice onions. Soak sliced cucumbers and onions 2 hours in salt brine, made of salt and water; drain. Combine vinegar, sugar, turmeric, celery seed, and mustard seed and bring to a boil. Remove from heat, add cucumbers and onions. Bring to boiling and cook 10 minutes. Pack into hot, sterilized jars, filling to within ½ inch of top. Seal at once.

Squash Fritters
Miriam Satz

1 winter squash or 2 medium summer squashes, mashed
1 egg, beaten
1 tablespoon onion, minced
2 tablespoons milk
½ cup flour
salt and pepper
1 teaspoon baking powder
olive oil

Mix squash, egg, onion, milk, flour, salt, pepper, and baking powder and stir. Drop batter by the spoonful into hot oil and fry 2–3 minutes until golden brown. Turn each fritter once. Remove to paper toweling.

Zucchini with Pasta
Miriam Satz

1 medium zucchini
3 tablespoons olive oil
¼ teaspoon oregano
¾ pound Spaghetti, linguini, etc.
1 tablespoon salt or less
1 clove garlic, minced
¼ teaspoon dried parsley flakes
Parmesan cheese

Peel squash and cut into julienne strips. Salt thoroughly and place in strainer to drain. Pat dry with paper toweling. Heat olive oil and sauté zucchini and garlic; add seasonings. Cook pasta according to package directions; drain and arrange on serving platter or individual serving dishes. Spoon zucchini mixture onto hot pasta. Sprinkle with Parmesan cheese.

Zucchini-Bean Stir-Fry
Miriam Satz

2 tablespoons peanut oil
3 cups zucchini, sliced or chopped
1 tablespoon lemon juice
sesame seeds
1 tablespoon cornstarch
1 pound fresh green beans, snapped into 2-inch pieces
¼ cup celery, chopped
1½ tablespoons salt or less
⅓ cup chicken stock or bouillon

Heat oil in heavy skillet or wok. Stir-fry beans 2–3 minutes, until cooked but still somewhat crisp. Add zucchini, celery, lemon juice, and seasonings. Stir-fry 3 minutes. Add stock; cover and lower heat. Simmer 3 minutes. Moisten cornstarch with 1 tablespoon of the stock; add to mixture. Stir until vegetables are glazed.
Serves 4

Zucchini-Spaghetti Soup
Miriam Satz

1 medium onion, minced
¼ cup olive oil
1 tomato, peeled and chopped
½ teaspoon basil
4 cups vegetable stock or chicken broth
1 clove garlic, minced
1½ pounds small zucchini, thinly sliced (4 medium)
salt and pepper
½ pound uncooked spaghetti

Sauté onion and garlic in olive oil in large saucepan. Add zucchini rounds, tomato, seasonings, and stock. Cover and simmer over low heat 1½ hours. Add short lengths of uncooked spaghetti and continue simmering another 10 minutes.
Serves 4

Spanish Rice
Miriam Satz
Mexican dish

1 cup rice. Put in skillet, cover with Mazola oil. Cook until rice is golden brown. Drip oil out of pan and set rice aside. Put ¼ cup grated onion, piece of garlic, grated, 1½ tablespoons tomato paste and 1 cup boiling water. Add salt and sugar to taste. When boiling, add rice and cook until done, about 25 minutes.

Paella
Miriam Satz
Mexican dish

Add cooked fish or cooked chicken (pieces) in the above recipe, if desired.

Potato Latkes
Miriam Satz

6 potatoes, grated
7 tablespoons Matzo meal or flour
2 eggs, beaten
¼ teaspoon baking powder
1 grated onion
2½ tablespoons olive oil
1 teaspoon salt

Mix all ingredients and sauté in olive oil in skillet. Serve with sour cream and apple sauce.

Home-Made Grape Juice Fresh From Garden
Miriam Satz

Pick grapes, wash, sort out unwanted grapes, discard stems as well. Place in large pot and cover with water. Cook about 10 minutes until grapes are mushy. Drain. Place grapes in food mill and crush them. Measure grape juice and use thin canning syrup—4 cups water with ¼ cup sugar (or more) boiled. Place grape juice and syrup in large heavy pot. When juice comes to a boil, fill sterilized jars to ½ inch from top. Use waterbath for 10 minutes. Seal. Let stand on towel for 24 hours before storing in cool place.

Home-Made Applesauce
Miriam Satz

Three pounds apples (Jonathon, Cortland, or Macintosh). Do not peel apples but quarter them and place in large heavy pot. Add 1 cup cold water, small amount of sugar and a little cinnamon. Cook until the apples are mushy and then use the food mill to crush them. Let the applesauce cool a bit and fill plastic containers for the freezer. (Jonathon and Cortland apples only appear in October so I make my applesauce then.)

Home-Made Raspberry Jam
Miriam Satz
All our children's favorite jam.

Pick raspberries from garden. Since there aren't enough for 1 batch of jam, I freeze them in plastic containers and save enough for 1 recipe. Then wash them, crush and measure raspberries. Follow the Light Sure-Jell directions. After filling sterilized jars, put in water bath for 5 minutes. Take out, place on towel and keep at room temperature for 24 hours before storing in a cool place.

Home-Made Frozen Strawberries
Miriam Satz

Pick fresh strawberries at neighborhood farms or buy them fresh at stores. Wash and slice some for the freezer. Place in small plastic containers and sprinkle a little sugar over the berries.

Strawberry Jam
Miriam Satz

Wash berries, crush them, and put in measuring cup. Follow Light Sure-Jell directions. Place in water bath and boil for 5 minutes. Take out and place on towel. Set at room temperature for 24 hours before storing.

Freezer Raspberry and Strawberry Jams
Miriam Satz

Jams made for the freezer have a real fresh fruit taste. Follow freezer directions from the Light Sure-Jell package.

Grape Jam
Miriam Satz

The juice can be used for making the freezer jam and the cooked jam by following the Light-Sure Jell directions.

Open House Punch
Miriam Satz
Used by Bloomsburg University.

Use cranberry juice and orange sherbet. Add ice and orange slices. Stir gently.

Green Colored Punch
Miriam Satz

Boil together for 3 minutes:
3 cups sugar
1½ cups water
green coloring
3 sticks of cinnamon

Cool. Add:
2 cups water
1 large can pineapple juice
2 cans frozen lemon juice
gingerale

Thoenen's Punch
Miriam Satz

Mix equal parts of Sauterne and White Champagne. Then add green ice (sherbet). Stir gently.

Baked Goods

Banana Bread
Miriam Satz
Easy recipe.

½ cup shortening
1 cup sugar
2 eggs, beaten
3 ripe bananas (crushed)
2 cups flour
1 teaspoon soda
¾ cup chopped nuts

Put batter in greased loaf pan and bake in moderate oven (350°) for about 1 hour. Do not cook too fast. Turn upside down to cool. Slice later.

Zucchini Bread
Miriam Satz

3 eggs, slightly beaten
1 cup salad oil
1 cup sugar
2 cups zucchini, grated and drained
3¼ cups flour
1 teaspoon baking powder
1 teaspoon baking soda
3 teaspoons cinnamon
1 teaspoon salt
¾ cup golden raisins
1 cup chopped nuts
1 cup chopped dates (optional)

Mix eggs, oil, sugar, zucchini, and vanilla together. Sift dry ingredients; combine with zucchini mixture. Add golden raisins, nuts, and dates. Makes 2 loaves. Bake at 350° for 1 hour; cool 10 minutes. Remove from pan. You may substitute ½ cup coarse bran for ½ cup flour.
Makes 2 loaves

Zucchini Walnut Bread
Miriam Satz

2 cups zucchini, grated (unpeeled)
3 eggs
¾–1 cup oil
1½ cups sugar
grated rind of 1 lemon (or 1/4 teaspoon lemon extract)

grated rind of 1 orange (or ¼ teaspoon orange
   extract)
1 teaspoon vanilla
3 cups flour
1 teaspoon salt
1 teaspoon baking soda
¼ teaspoon baking powder
2 teaspoons cinnamon
½ cup chopped walnuts
dates (optional)

Preheat oven to 350°. Beat eggs; add oil and sugar. Mix. Add rinds, vanilla, and zucchini; mix well. In a separate bowl, mix flour, salt, baking powder, and soda, cinnamon, nuts, and dates. Add and mix well to zucchini mixture. Grease 2 loaf pans. Bake for 1 hour and 10 minutes. Cool and then remove from pans.

Pineapple Zucchini Bread
Miriam Satz

3 eggs
1 cup oil (canola)
1½ cups sugar
2 teaspoons vanilla
2 cups zucchini, grated
1 (8½-ounce) can drained, crushed pineapple
3 cups flour
2 teaspoons baking soda
1 teaspoon salt
½ teaspoon baking powder
1½ teaspoons cinnamon
¾ teaspoon nutmeg
½ cup golden raisins
½ cup chopped walnuts

Blend all ingredients. Pour into two well greased loaf pans. Bake at 350° for 1 hour.

Variation:
Use 2 cups flour with 1 teaspoon cinnamon. Omit nutmeg and pineapple.

Zucchini Muffins
Miriam Satz

3 cups flour
1 teaspoon baking powder
1 teaspoon soda
1 teaspoon cinnamon
⅔ cup sugar
4 eggs (room temp.)
1 cup oil
1 teaspoon vanilla
2 cups grated, unpeeled zucchini
   (about 12 ounces)
½ cup chopped walnuts
½ cup golden raisins

Heat oven to 350°. Grease muffin pans. Sift first four ingredients; set aside. Combine sugar and eggs; beat at medium speed for 2 minutes. Gradually add oil slow and steady, beating constantly, for 3 minutes. Add zucchini (peeled or unpeeled) and vanilla, blending well (this can be done by hand if you prefer). Stir in nuts and raisins. Fold in dry ingredients; do not overbeat, just stir until all is well blended. Fill pans ⅔ full. Bake at 350° for 20–25 minutes. Cool on rack.
Makes 24

Cinnamon Twists
Miriam Satz

1 cup milk
3 tablespoons sugar
1 teaspoon salt
1 cake yeast (or 1 package dry yeast)
1 egg
2 tablespoons very soft margarine
  or shortening
3 cups or a little more, flour

Heat milk until lukewarm. Crumble in yeast, then add sugar, salt, egg, margarine, and flour. Mix well; roll out into 2 oblong pieces. Spread with tablespoonful soft margarine. Sprinkle half of dough with mixture of ⅓ cup sugar (brown, if desired) and 1 teaspoonful cinnamon. Fold other half over. Cut into 1 inch strips. Twist each piece. Place on greased baking sheet. Cover and let rise 1 hour, then bake at 375° for about 15 minutes.

Fresh Blueberry Cobbler
Miriam Satz

½ cup sugar
4 cups fresh blueberries
1 cup cold water
1 tablespoon cornstarch
1 teaspoon lemon juice

Blend ½ cup sugar and the cornstarch in small saucepan. Add 1 cup cold water. Stir in blueberries and lemon juice. Cook, stirring constantly, until mixture thickens and boils. Boil and stir 1 minute. Pour mixture into 2-quart casserole.

Heat oven to 400°. Stir together 1 cup flour, 1 tablespoon sugar, 1½ teaspoon baking powder, and ½ teaspoon salt. Add 3 tablespoons shortening and ½ cup milk. Cut through shortening with fork 6 times; mix until dough forms a ball. Drop mixture by spoonfuls onto hot fruit. Bake 25 to 30 minutes or until biscuit topping is golden brown. Serve warm, and if desired, with cream or frozen yogurt.

Variation:
Use different combinations of fruit such as fresh rhubarb, strawberries, pears, and raspberries.

Oil Pastry
Miriam Satz

1¾ cups flour
½ cup salad oil
1 teaspoon salt
3 to 4 tablespoons cold water

Measure flour and salt into mixing bowl. Add oil; mix with fork until particles are size of small peas. Sprinkle in water, 1 tablespoon at a time, mixing with fork until flour is moistened and dough almost cleans side of bowl (1 to 2 tablespoons oil can be added if needed). Gather dough together with hands (or wax paper); press firmly into a ball. Roll pastry between two pieces of wax paper.

Baked Pie Shell: Prick bottom and side thoroughly with fork to prevent puffing while shell bakes. Bake at 475° for 8 to 10 minutes. Cool before filling.

Makes 1 10-inch one crust pie or 8- or 9-inch two-crust pie

Fresh Pumpkin Pie
Miriam Satz

Famous Libby's recipe.
2 eggs, slightly beaten
1¾ or 2 cups fresh pumpkin cooked and mashed
**   or canned pumpkin**
¾ cup sugar
½ teaspoon salt
1 teaspoon cinnamon
½ teaspoon ginger
¼ teaspoon cloves
1 cup evaporated milk and ⅓ cup milk
**   mixed together**

Mix ingredients in the order given above. Pour pumpkin mixture into unbaked pie crust. Bake in hot oven (450°) 10 minutes. Reduce temperature to moderate (350°) and bake 20 minutes. Before completing baking, cover with the following pecan topping.

Melt 1 tablespoon brown sugar and 2 tablespoons butter or margarine in saucepan. Add ½ cup pecan meats. Place on top of pie. Continue baking in moderate oven (350°) 20 to 30 minutes or until a silver knife comes out clean when inserted in filling.

French Apple Pie
Miriam Satz

pastry for 9-inch one-crust pie
½ cup sugar
½ teaspoon nutmeg
dash of salt
¼ cup flour
1 teaspoon cinnamon
6 cups thinly sliced pared tart apples
**   (about 5 medium)**

Place all ingredients in unbaked pie crust.

Topping:
Mix 1 cup flour, ½ cup butter or margarine, ½ cup brown sugar (packed), with fork or pastry blender until crumbly. Place mixture on top of pie. Bake in 425° oven for 50 minutes. Cover crumb topping with foil last 10 minutes of baking if top browns too quickly.

Deep Dish Fresh Fruit Pie
Miriam Satz
Stephanie's favorite

1 quart fresh rhubarb, sliced
½ pint raspberries
3 fresh pears cut in pieces
½ pint strawberries
½ blueberries

Place the above fruit in a large bowl. Mix the following ingredients in another bowl:

1⅓ to 1½ cups sugar
⅓ cup flour
½ teaspoon grated orange peel, if desired or ¼
**   teaspoon orange extract**

Stir the above mixture onto the fruit. Mix gently. Place fruit mixture into an oblong 9 x 13 inch baking dish. Dot with 2 tablespoons butter or margarine. Cover with a 10-inch pie crust. Cut slits on top. Bake in a 425° oven for 45 to 50 minutes or until crust is nicely browned and juice begins to bubble through slits. (Can place pie on cookie sheet before baking so there will be no spills.)

Blueberry Cheese Pie
Miriam Satz

1 3-ounce package cream cheese
½ teaspoon vanilla
1 can blueberry filling
1 9-inch graham cracker crust pie shell
½ cup powdered sugar
½ pint whipping cream
1 tablespoon lemon juice

Cream together the cream cheese, sugar, and vanilla. Whip cream until stiff but not dry. Fold whipped cream into cheese. Turn onto graham cracker pie crust. Mix lemon juice into pie filling and spoon over cream. Chill before serving.
Serves 8

Blueberry-Cheesecake Dessert
Miriam Satz

16 graham crackers, crushed
½ cup butter, melted
½ cup sugar

Mix above ingredients and put in 9 x 13 inch pan and bake for 3 minutes at 375°.

2 8-ounce packages of cream cheese
4 eggs
1 cup sugar

Beat above ingredients and then spread on top of above mixture and bake 25 minutes. Let cool.

2 cans blueberries, drained
2½ tablespoons cornstarch
½ cup sugar
2 tablespoons lemon juice

Mix cornstarch and sugar, add juice drained from blueberries, cook until thick. Let cool until completely cold. Carefully fold in blueberries and lemon juice. Spread on top of cheesecake. Add whipped cream and serve.

Cheese Cake
Miriam Satz

Crust:
¼ pound butter
6 tablespoons sugar
2 eggs
1½ cups flour
¾ teaspoon baking powder
½ teaspoon salt

Grease pan with butter. Spread in corners of pan, place in refrigerator while making filling.

Filling:
12-ounce package cream cheese
¾ cup sugar
3 yolks, beat whites separately
½ juice of lemon
1 teaspoon vanilla
3 tablespoons flour

Beat with mixer at low speed. Then add 2 cups milk very slowly. Add egg whites last. Pour into crust and sprinkle with cinnamon. You may use crushed pineapple in bottom and then put filling on top. Bake one hour in 350° oven.

Apple Coffee Cake
Miriam Satz

3 eggs
1⅓ cup sugar
½ cup oil
2 cups flour
1 teaspoon baking powder
½ teaspoon soda
½ teaspoon salt
1 teaspoon vanilla

Combine eggs, sugar, oil, and vanilla. Add dry ingredients alternately with juice of ½ lemon (1 tablespoon) and ½ orange (¼). Spread ½ mixture in large baking dish. Spread with 6 sliced apples that have been mixed with ¼ cup sugar and ½ teaspoon cinnamon. Add remaining batter and bake 1 hour in 350° oven.

Jewish Apple Cake
Miriam Satz

3 cups unsifted flour
1 cup cooking oil
¼ cup orange-pineapple juice
3 teaspoons baking powder
sugar and cinnamon mixture
2 cups sugar
4 eggs
2½ teaspoons vanilla
1 teaspoon salt
4 large apples, pared and sliced

Place all ingredients except apples and sugar-cinnamon in a large bowl and beat until smooth. Pour half the batter into ungreased tube or large baking dish. Spread half the apple slices over the batter. Sprinkle with half of sugar and cinnamon (1 teaspoon cinnamon mixed with ¾ cup sugar).

Add remaining batter. Top with rest of apples and sprinkle with sugar-cinnamon. Bake in preheated 350° oven about 1½ hours or until done.

Best All Around Cake: Golden Layer Cake
Miriam Satz

sift together in bowl:
2¼ cups sifted flour
1½ cups sugar
3 teaspoons baking powder
1 teaspoon salt

Add:
½ cup soft shortening
⅔ cup milk
1½ teaspoons vanilla

Beat 2 minutes. Add another ⅓ cup milk, 2 eggs, beat 2 more minutes. Pour into prepared pans. Bake for 30 minutes in 350° oven. Best with broiled icing, peanut butter icing, or cocoa icing.

Mix:
⅓ cup soft butter
⅔ cup brown sugar
¼ cup rich cream or milk
½ cup nuts, cut up
½ cup coconut

Spread over top of warm cake. Place low under broiler until icing browns. Watch!

Peanut Butter Icing
Miriam Satz

Stir together until creamy:
¼ cup chunk style peanut butter
3 cups sifted confectioners sugar
¼ to ⅓ cup warm milk

Cocoa Icing
Miriam Satz

2 cups confectioner's sugar
2 big lumps butter or margarine
1 egg yolk, well beaten
2 tablespoons cocoa

Soften butter, combine all ingredients, add cream or warm milk to make right consistency. Beat well.

Marble Cake
Miriam Satz

1 cup shortening
2 cups sugar (or less)
4 eggs
3 cups flour
4 teaspoons baking powder
¾ teaspoon salt
¼ teaspoon almond extract
1 cup milk
1 teaspoon vanilla
2 squares (2 ounces) unsweetened chocolate
3 tablespoons boiling water
⅛ teaspoon baking soda

Cream together shortening and sugar. Add eggs 1 at a time, beating after each. Sift together flour, baking powder, and salt. Add alternately with milk to creamed mixture. Add vanilla. Melt chocolate over hot water; add water and soda. Divide batter in ½; to ½ add chocolate mixture and almond extract. Place batters by alternate spoonfuls in greased 9" tube pan or 9 x 13 inch oblong pan. Bake in moderate oven (350°) 1¼ hours. Cool 10 minutes. Remove cake from pan; cool on wire rack. Best with Fudge Icing.

Fudge Icing
Miriam Satz

1 square chocolate
2 tablespoons milk
1 teaspoon vanilla
⅓ cup margarine
confectioners sugar

Cook over low heat (over water) and stir until it gets to be thick, like chocolate pudding. Stir in powdered sugar until right consistency. Add vanilla. Thin mixture with water or milk, if necessary.

Creamy Vanilla Frosting
Miriam Satz

In a saucepan combine 2 tablespoons water, ¼ cup sugar, and ¼ teaspoon salt and boil for 1 minute. Then blend with 2½ cups confectioners sugar and 1 egg. Add ½ cup shortening and 1 teaspoon vanilla and beat until frosting is smooth and creamy.
Makes lots of frosting

Chocolate Vanilla Frosting
Miriam Satz

To recipe above add 2 squares unsweetened chocolate melted, along with the vanilla.

Chocolate Cake
Miriam Satz

Combine in mixing bowl:
1¼ cups sugar
1 teaspoon soda
1½ cups cake flour
1 teaspoon salt
½ teaspoon baking powder

Add and beat by hand or mixer (medium speed) for 2 minutes:
½ cup shortening
2 squares melted unsweetened chocolate
¾ cup milk

Add and beat for 2 minutes longer:
2 eggs
1 teaspoon vanilla
⅓ cup milk

Baking time for layers 30 to 35 minutes or longer for 9 x 13 inch oblong pan.

Simple Cocoa Icing
Miriam Satz
Good on pound cakes.

Mix together:
½ cup confectioners sugar
2 tablespoons cocoa
2 tablespoons water
1 teaspoon vanilla or other flavoring

Penuche Icing
Miriam Satz

1½ cups brown sugar
⅜ cup shortening or butter
⅜ cup milk
¼ teaspoon salt

Bring slowly to a full rolling boil, stirring constantly, and boil 1 minute. Remove from heat and beat until lukewarm. Add ¾ teaspoon vanilla and continue beating until thick enough to spread. Add about 1 teaspoon cream. One-half cup chopped nuts may be placed on top.

Wacky Chocolate Cake
Miriam Satz
No eggs or milk.

3 cups flour
2 cups sugar
2 teaspoons soda
6 tablespoons cocoa
1 teaspoon salt

Sift into ungreased pan, 9 x 13 inch, and make 3 holes in it and add:

2 tablespoons cider vinegar
2 teaspoons vanilla
10 tablespoons melted butter or cooking oil

Pour 2 cups cold water into this and beat. Bake at 350° oven for 40 to 45 minutes. Use Peanut Butter Icing or Easy Caramel Frosting.

Easy Caramel Frosting
Miriam Satz

½ cup butter or margarine
¼ cup milk
1 teaspoon vanilla
1 cup brown sugar, packed
about 2 cups sifted confectioner's sugar

Melt butter or margarine in saucepan, stir in brown sugar. Cook and stir over low heat 2 minutes. Add milk, continue stirring until boiling. Remove from heat. Cool to lukewarm. Put in small mixing bowl. Add sugar and vanilla while beating on No. 2 speed. Then beat on No. 11 speed until spreading consistency about 2 minutes. May add few drops of hot water or more sugar as needed. Spread on cake at once. Sprinkle with chopped nuts, if desired.

Wacky Chocolate Cake #2
Miriam Satz
Martin's favorite—½ recipe of Wacky Cake recipe

1½ cups sifted flour
3 tablespoons cocoa
1 teaspoon soda
1 cup sugar
½ teaspoon salt
5 tablespoons cooking oil
1 tablespoon vinegar
1 teaspoon vanilla
1 cup cold water

Follow directions from Wacky cake #1. Frost with White Icing. Popular with the Satz family.

White Icing
Miriam Satz
Use ½ recipe for this cake.

Cook:
½ cup milk
2½ tablespoons cornstarch

Stir constantly. Cool. Add:
1½ cups confectioners sugar
½ cup shortening (Crisco)
¼ teaspoon salt
½ vanilla

Use electric mixer. Sprinkle top with chocolate, coconut bits, or crushed nuts.

Brown Sugar Meringue Frosting
Miriam Satz

1 cup light brown sugar, firmly packed
⅓ cup water
¼ teaspoon cream of tartar
2 egg whites

In saucepan combine sugar, water, and cream of tartar. Boil rapidly until syrup spins a thread or to 230°. Beat the egg whites until stiff. Then gradually beat in hot syrup and continue beating until the frosting is thick. Spread on layer cake, oblong cake, or cupcakes in attractive swirls.

Quick-Method Spice Cake
Miriam Satz

Combine in mixing bowl:
2⅓ cups sifted cake flour
1 cup sugar
¾ cup brown sugar
1 teaspoon salt

1 teaspoon baking powder
¾ teaspoon soda
1 teaspoon ginger
¼ teaspoon each of clove and cinnamon

Add:
½ cup shortening (Crisco)
¾ cup buttermilk

Beat vigorously for 2 minutes by hand or mixer (medium speed). Add:
3 eggs
¼ cup buttermilk

Beat for 2 minutes longer. Pour batter into prepared pans (2 9-inch layers or 13 x 9 inch oblong pan) and bake at 350° for 35 to 40 minutes. Use Brown Sugar Meringue Frosting or broiled icings.

Oatmeal Spice Cake
Miriam Satz

1½ cups flour
1 cup brown sugar (packed)
1½ teaspoons soda
½ teaspoon salt
½ cup shortening (Crisco)
2 eggs
1 cup quick-cooking oats (packed)
½ cup sugar
1 teaspoon cinnamon
½ teaspoon nutmeg
1 cup water
2 tablespoons dark molasses

Heat oven to 350°. Grease and flour baking pan, 13 x 9 x 2 inches. Measure all ingredients in large mixing bowl. Blend ½ minute on low speed, scraping bowl constantly. Beat 3 minutes high speed, scraping bowl occasionally. Pour into pan.

Bake 35 to 40 minutes or until wooden pick inserted in center comes out clean. Cool slightly. Spread topping over cake. Peanut Butter Broiled Topping works well.

Peanut Butter Broiled Topping
Miriam Satz

¼ cup soft butter or margarine
3 tablespoons milk
¼ cup peanut butter
⅔ cup brown sugar (packed)
1 cup peanuts, finely chopped (optional)

Mix together and frost cake, baked. Broil until slightly brown.

White Cake with Grated Chocolate (Ski Cake)
Miriam Satz
Martin's choice

Grease and flour two (8 or 9 inch) layer pans or 13 x 9 x 2 oblong) pan.

Sift together into bowl:
2 cups flour
1½ cups sugar
3½ teaspoons baking powder
1 teaspoon salt

Add:
½ cup shortening
1 cup milk
¼ square unsweetened chocolate grated
1 teaspoon vanilla
4 egg whites (unbeaten)

Pour into prepared pans. Bake until cake is done in 350° oven for 30 minutes in layer pans or 35 to 40 minutes in oblong pan. Frost with Egg Yolk Icing and Melted Chocolate Chips.

Egg Yolk Icing
Miriam Satz

½ cup butter or margarine
1½ cups confectioners sugar
3 egg yolks
chocolate chips

Work butter until creamy, then add confectioners sugar and egg yokes and mix well. Frost cake on top and between layers. Melt chocolate chips with 1 tablespoonful milk. Pour over top of cake and spread lightly.
Very attractive birthday cake.

Dinette Cake
Miriam Satz
Miriam's choice

1¼ cups flour
1½ teaspoons baking powder
¾ cup milk
1 egg
1 cup sugar (or less)
½ teaspoon salt
⅓ cup shortening (Crisco)
1 teaspoon vanilla

Heat oven to 350°. Grease and flour "heart-shaped" pan, 8 x 8 x 2 or 9 x 9 x 2 inches. Measure all ingredients into large mixing bowl. Blend ½ minute on low speed, scraping bowl constantly. Beat 3 minutes high speed, scraping bowl occasionally. Pour into pan. Bake 35 to 40 minutes. Cool. Use White Icing or Richmond Chocolate Frosting.

Richmond Chocolate Frosting
Miriam Satz

½ cup sugar
1½ tablespoons cornstarch
1 1-ounce square unsweetened chocolate, grated
dash of salt
½ cup boiling water
1½ tablespoons butter or margarine
½ teaspoon vanilla

Mix sugar and cornstarch; add chocolate and salt. Add water; cook until mixture thickens. Remove from heat; add butter and vanilla. Spread on cake while hot for a glossy frosting which remains soft and smooth. Great for brownies.

Blintz Torte
Miriam Satz
Ron's choice

½ cup shortening
½ cup sugar
⅛ teaspoon salt
4 egg yolks, beaten lightly
1 teaspoon vanilla
3 tablespoons milk
1 cup cake flour
1 teaspoon baking powder
4 egg whites
¾ cup sugar
½ cup sliced, blanched almonds, pecans, or
    walnuts
1 tablespoon sugar
½ teaspoon cinnamon

Cream shortening; beat in sugar and salt, egg yolks, vanilla, milk, and flour, sifted with baking powder. Spread mixture in 2 round greased cake pans. Beat egg whites until very light. Add ¾ cup sugar gradually and spread on the unbaked mixture in both pans. Sprinkle with almonds or other nuts, 1 tablespoonful sugar and cinnamon and bake in 350° oven about 30 minutes. Let cool and put together with cream filling.

Cream Filling:
⅓ **cup sugar**
3 **tablespoons cornstarch**
¼ **teaspoon salt**
1 **teaspoon vanilla**
2 **egg yolks**
2 **tablespoons butter or margarine**
2 **cups milk**

Combine sugar, cornstarch, salt, and egg yolks. Beat thoroughly. Add butter and enough milk to make a smooth paste. Add paste to remaining hot milk and cook over boiling water, stirring constantly until mixture is thickened. Cool and add vanilla. If desired, add ½ cup chopped nuts.
Makes one (9 inch) 2 layer cake
Very pretty to look at and tastes delicious.

Hawaiian Pineapple Cake
Miriam Satz
Barry's choice

Grease generously and flour 2 8-inch layer pans or 13 x 9 pan.

Sift together:
1¾ **cup flour**
1⅛ **cups sugar**
3 **teaspoons baking powder**
1 **teaspoon salt**

Add:
⅓ **cup shortening (Crisco)**
1 **cup milk**
½ **teaspoon lemon flavoring**
½ **teaspoon vanilla**
2 **egg yolks and 1 whole egg**

Beat 2 minutes in mixer. Add egg yolks and whole egg. Beat 2 minutes more. Pour into prepared pans. Bake in 350° oven 30 to 35 minutes for layers and 35 to 40 minutes for oblong pan. Cool. Place Pineapple Filling between layers and save some for the center of the top layer. Use Fluffy White Frosting for the rest of the top and sides.

Pineapple Filling:
Mix in saucepan:
½ **cup sugar**
3 **tablespoons cornstarch**
½ **teaspoon salt**

Add:
¾ **cup pineapple juice**
1 **cup crushed pineapple, well drained**
1 **tablespoon butter or margarine**
1 **teaspoon lemon juice**

Boil mixture for 1 minute. Cool thoroughly.
Tastes as good as it looks.

Fluffy White Frosting
Miriam Satz

Combine 1 egg white, ⅔ cup sugar, ¼ cup light corn syrup, 3 tablespoons water, ⅛ teaspoon salt, and ⅛ teaspoon cream of tartar. Place in top of double boiler over rapidly boiling water and beat with rotary beater until mixture stands in peaks. Remove from boiling water. Add 1 teaspoon vanilla; continue beating until thick enough to spread. Frost sides and top of cooled cake.

Bonnie Butter Cake
Miriam Satz
Stephanie's choice

⅔ cup butter or margarine, softened
1½ teaspoons vanilla
2½ teaspoons baking powder
1 teaspoon salt
1¾ cups sugar (or less)
2 eggs
3 cups cake flour or 2¾ cups flour
1½ cups milk

Heat oven to 350°. Grease and flour baking pan, 13 x 9 x 2 inches, or two 9-inch or three 8-inch round layer pans. In large mixer bowl, mix butter, sugar, eggs, and vanilla until fluffy. Beat 5 minutes on high speed, scraping bowl occasionally. On low speed, mix in flour, baking powder, and salt alternately with milk. Pour into pan(s). Bake oblong 45 to 50 minutes, layers 30 to 35 minutes. Cool. Frost cake with French Silk Frosting.

French Silk Frosting
Miriam Satz

2⅔ cups confectioners sugar
2 ounces melted unsweetened chocolate (cool)
⅔ cup soft butter or margarine
¾ teaspoon vanilla

In small mixer bowl, blend sugar, butter, chocolate, and vanilla on low speed. Gradually add milk; beat until smooth and fluffy.

Banana-Nut Cake
Miriam Satz
Madelyn's choice; sent to her in college for her birthday for some years.

2¼ cups cake flour
1¼ teaspoons baking powder
1 teaspoon salt
⅔ cup buttermilk
1¼ cups mashed ripe bananas
1⅔ cups sugar
1¼ teaspoons soda
⅔ cup shortening (Crisco)
3 eggs
⅔ cup finely chopped nuts

Heat oven to 350°. Grease and flour baking pan, 13 x 9 x 2 inches, or two 9-inch or three 8-inch round layer pans. Measure all ingredients into large mixer bowl. Blend ½ minute on low speed, scraping bowl constantly. Beat 3 minutes high speed, scraping bowl occasionally. Pour into pan(s). Bake oblong 45 to 50 minutes, layers 35 to 40 minutes. Cool. Frost with Butterscotch Icing.

Butterscotch Icing
Miriam Satz

1 cup brown sugar
¼ cup milk
2 tablespoons butter or margarine
1 tablespoon light corn syrup
¼ cup shortening
2 cups sifted confectioners' sugar
¼ teaspoon salt
3 tablespoons hot milk

Cook first 4 ingredients to 250° or until a small amount of the syrup forms a hard ball when dropped into cold water. Stir constantly after mixture begins to boil. Remove from heat. Combine shortening and salt and add sugar gradually, creaming well. Add hot milk, then add hot butterscotch mixture gradually and beat until smooth and thick enough to spread. Can sprinkle crushed nuts on top.

Assorted Cookie Recipes

Bar Cookies: Brownies
Miriam Satz

Melt together over hot water:
2 squares unsweetened chocolate (2 ounces)
⅓ cup shortening (Crisco)

Beat in:
1 cup sugar
2 eggs
½ teaspoon vanilla

Sift together and stir in:
¾ cup flour
½ teaspoon baking powder
½ teaspoon salt

Mix in:
½ cup broken nuts

Spread in well-greased 8-inch square pan. Bake until top has dull crust. A slight imprint will be left when top is touched lightly with finger. Cool slightly, then cut into squares (16 2" squares). Use 350° oven for 30 to 35 minutes. Frost with Marie's Chocolate Icing.
The best.

Marie's Chocolate Icing
Miriam Satz

Melt over hot water 1 tablespoon butter or margarine and 1 square unsweetened chocolate (1 ounce). Blend in 1½ tablespoons warm water. Stir and beat in about 1 cup sifted confectioner's sugar until icing will spread easily.

Cocoa Brownies
Miriam Satz

½ cup shortening
1 cup sugar
2 eggs
1 teaspoon vanilla
⅔ cup flour
½ cup cocoa
½ teaspoon baking powder
½ teaspoon salt
½ cup chopped walnuts

Heat oven to 350°. Mix shortening, sugar, eggs, and vanilla until well blended. Sift dry ingredients; mix in. Stir in nuts. Spread in well-greased pan, 8 x 8 x 2. Bake about 30 minutes. Cool; cut in 2" squares. Frost with Butter Frosting or Mocha Frosting.
Makes 16 brownies

Butter Frosting
Miriam Satz

¼ cup butter or margarine
2 cups confectioner's sugar
⅛ salt
3 tablespoons warm milk
1 teaspoon vanilla

Cream butter until soft. Slowly stir in 1 cup sugar and the salt. Add additional sugar alternately with warm milk, beating thoroughly after each addition until creamy and smooth. Beat in vanilla. Additional milk may be added to give frosting spreading consistency. For brownies use one-half of this recipe.

Variation:
Substitute coffee for milk. Add 1½ tablespoons cocoa with the creamed butter.

Cinnamon Frosted Zucchini Bars
Miriam Satz

1¾ cups flour
¾ cup butter or margarine
½ cup brown sugar
1 teaspoon vanilla
1 cup coconut
¾ chopped nuts
1½ teaspoon baking powder
½ cup sugar
2 eggs
2 cups shredded zucchini (peeled or unpeeled)

Grease 15 x 10 x 1 baking pan. In small mixing bowl stir together flour and baking powder; set aside. In large mixer bowl beat butter or margarine on medium speed for 30 seconds. Add sugars, beat until fluffy. Add eggs and vanilla; beat well. Stir in flour mixture. Stir in zucchini, coconut, and nuts. Bake in 350° oven for 30 minutes. Cool. Cut into bars. Use Cinnamon Frosting.
Makes 36 bars

Cinnamon Frosting
Miriam Satz

Mix 2 cups confectioners' sugar, 2 tablespoons warm milk, 2 tablespoons butter or margarine melted. Add ½ to 1 teaspoon cinnamon and 1 teaspoon vanilla. Beat until smooth.

Light Brownies
Miriam Satz
Easy to make.

½ cup butter or margarine
1½ cups light brown sugar
2 eggs
1 teaspoon vanilla
1½ cups flour
2 teaspoons baking powder
½ cup chopped nuts
2 tablespoons coconut

In a saucepan melt butter. Add sugar, eggs, and vanilla. Sift dry ingredients together and add to mixture in saucepan. Mix well. Use a greased 11 x 7 pan and bake in a 350° oven for 20 to 25 minutes. Cut bars diagonally.

Tutti Frutti Squares
Miriam Satz

Beat 2 eggs; gradually, beat in ¾ cup sugar. Stir in 1 cup each chopped walnuts and dates; ¾ cup diced mixed candied fruits, 3 tablespoons melted butter, ¾ cup flour, sifted with 1 teaspoon salt. Spread in waxed-paper-lined 7 x 11 x 1 greased pan. Bake at 325° (fairly slow) about 50 minutes, until firm to touch. Turn out, pull off paper. Cool, cut in squares, roll in confectioners' Powdered sugar.
Makes 40 chewy cookie squares

Date Bars
Miriam Satz

1 egg
½ cup sugar
½ cup melted shortening or salad oil
1 cup chopped pitted dates
¼ cup chopped walnuts meats
½ cup flour
½ teaspoon baking powder
¼ teaspoon salt
powdered sugar

Beat egg; add sugar; mix well. Add shortening or salad oil. Add dates and nut meats. Sift together flour, baking powder, and salt; add. Mix well. Spread in greased pan 8 x 8 x 2 inches. Bake in moderate oven (325°) 30 minutes. Cool; cut in bars. Roll in powdered sugar.

Congo Squares
Miriam Satz

2¾ cups flour
2½ teaspoons baking powder
½ teaspoon salt
⅔ cup shortening (half Mazola and half vegetable shortening)
½ teaspoon cinnamon
1 teaspoon vanilla
2¼ cups brown sugar
3 eggs
½ package chocolate chips
1 cup chopped nuts
½ cup coconut

Mix and sift flour, baking powder, salt, and cinnamon. Put shortening into bowl and add brown sugar. Stir until well mixed, then add eggs and mix. Add dry ingredients, then nuts, coconut, and chocolate chips. Pour into greased pan, 13 x 9 x 1, and bake 35 to 40 minutes at 350°.

Refrigerator Cookies

Oatmeal Crisps
Miriam Satz

1 cup shortening or 2 sticks margarine
2 eggs
1½ cups flour
1 teaspoon soda
½ cup chopped pecans or walnuts
1 cup brown sugar
1 cup sugar
1 teaspoon vanilla
1 teaspoon salt
3 cups quick oats
½ cup chopped dates

Mix all ingredients. Make rolls 1½ inches in diameter and wrap in waxed paper. Chill thoroughly. Slice ¼ inch thick and bake 10 minutes in a 350° oven.

Pinwheel Cookies
Miriam Satz

2 cups flour
1 teaspoon baking powder
¼ teaspoon salt
½ cup soft butter or margarine
1 cup firmly packed light brown sugar
1 egg
1 teaspoon vanilla
2 tablespoons cocoa

Sift flour, baking powder, and salt together. Cream butter and sugar thoroughly. Add egg and vanilla, beating until light. Gradually add flour mixture, beating until blended. Divide dough in half. Add cocoa to one half of dough. Roll each piece of dough on lightly floured waxed paper to form a 9 x 12-inch rectangle ¼ inch thick. Place chocolate layer on top of butterscotch layer, remove wax paper and roll up dough lengthwise to form a 12-inch roll. Wrap in wax paper; chill until firm. Slice cookies ¼ inch thick. Bake on lightly greased baking sheet in moderate oven 350° 10 to 12 minutes or until lightly browned.
Yield about 6 dozen cookies

Rolled Cookies

Hanukkah Cookies
Miriam Satz

2 cups flour
½ teaspoon salt
1 egg
¼ cup milk
1 cup sugar
2 teaspoons baking powder
⅓ cup butter or margarine
1 teaspoon vanilla

Cream butter and sugar in a large bowl. In another bowl, beat the egg and add the milk and flavoring. Stir both mixtures into a large bowl. Sift the flour, salt, and baking powder. Add these ingredients into the large mixture and stir well. Place the dough into the refrigerator for one hour. Dust a bread board and rolling pin with flour. Roll out the cool dough about ¼ inch thick. Cut with KTAV Cookie Cutters. Place on greased cookie sheet. Bake in 375° oven for about 8 minutes. Frost with flavored icing and decorate.

Peek-A-Boo Oatmeal Cookies
Miriam Satz

2½ cups flour
1 teaspoon soda
1 teaspoon salt
1 cup brown sugar
1 cup shortening, soft
½ cup water
2½ cups quick or old-fashioned oats
½ cup jelly or jam

Sift together flour, soda, and salt into bowl. Add sugar, shortening, and water. Beat until smooth, about 2 minutes. Fold in oats.

Sprinkle a bread board generously with confectioners' sugar. Roll dough very thin. Cut with cooky cutter. Cut a design in half the cookies (small ½ inch hole in center). Place plain cookies on lightly greased cooky sheet. Top with ½ teaspoon jelly and jam and cover with a designed (hole in center) cookie, lightly pressing edges together.

Bake in a moderate oven, 350°, 10 to 12 minutes.
Makes about 3½ dozen cookies
Pretty to look at and tasty.

Drop Cookies

Cocoa Drop Cookies
Miriam Satz

Mix thoroughly:
½ cup shortening (part butter or margarine)
1 egg
1 cup sugar

Stir in:
¾ cup buttermilk or sour milk
1 teaspoon vanilla

Sift together and stir in:
1¾ cup flour
½ teaspoon soda
½ teaspoon salt
½ cup cocoa

Mix in, if desired, 1 cup nuts, cut up, or raisins. Chill at least 1 hour. Drop rounded teaspoonfuls about 2 inches apart on lightly greased baking sheet. Bake just until, when touched lightly with finger, almost no imprint remains. Baking temperature is 400° and bake for 8 to 10 minutes.

Frost one-half of cookies with a vanilla butter icing and the other half with a cocoa icing. Place one-half small assorted gumdrops (cut in half) on top.
Very attractive for festive occasions.

Peanut Butter Cookies
Miriam Satz
Barry's favorite

Mix thoroughly:
½ **cup soft shortening (half Mazola oil and half vegetable shortening**
½ **cup sugar**
½ **cup brown sugar**
½ **cup peanut butter (smooth or chunky)**
1 **egg**

Sift together and stir in:
1¼ **cups flour**
½ **teaspoon baking powder**
¾ **teaspoon soda**
¼ **teaspoon salt**

Chill dough. Roll into balls (size of large walnut). Place 3 inches apart on lightly greased baking sheet. Flatten with fork dipped in flour…crisscross. Bake in 375° oven for 10 to 12 minutes.

Brown Sugar Pecan Rounds
Miriam Satz

½ **cup butter or margarine**
1¼ **cups brown sugar (packed)**
1 **egg**
1¼ **cups flour**
¼ **teaspoon soda**
⅛ **teaspoon salt**
½ **cup coarsely chopped pecans**

Heat oven to 350° (moderate). Cream butter and brown sugar thoroughly. Beat egg in well. Sift flour with dry ingredients and blend in. Stir in pecans. Drop ½ to 1 teaspoonful dough 2" apart on greased baking sheet. (Cookies flatten and spread.) Bake 7 to 8 minutes.

Gingersnap Cookies
Miriam Satz
Miriam's favorite

⅔ **cup shortening (half Mazola oil and half vegetable shortening, Crisco)**
2 **cups flour**
1 **cup sugar**
¼ **cup light molasses**
1 **beaten egg**
1 **teaspoon ginger**
¼ **teaspoon salt**
2 **teaspoons soda**
1 **teaspoon cinnamon**
1 **teaspoon cloves**

Cream shortening and sugar; add molasses and egg and beat well. Add sifted dry ingredients, mix well. Roll in small balls, flatten with fork and sprinkle lightly with sugar. Place 2 inches apart on greased cookie sheet. Bake in 375° oven for 8 to 10 minutes.
Makes 4½ dozen

Corn Meal Cookies
Miriam Satz

1 **cup shortening**
2 **eggs**
½ **cup raisins, chopped**
1 **teaspoon baking powder**
½ **teaspoon salt**
1½ **cups sugar (or less)**
1 **teaspoon lemon extract**
3 **cups cake flour**
1 **teaspoon nutmeg**
1 **cup yellow corn meal**

Cream shortening, add sugar, eggs, and lemon extract. Beat well. Dredge raisins with ½ cup of flour and add. Sift remaining flour with other dry ingredients and add, mixing thoroughly. Drop by teaspoons onto a greased cookie sheet and flatten out with a fork. Bake 10 to 12 minutes at 400°. They keep very well.

Variations:
Increase raisins to 1 cup and add ½ cup finely chopped nuts. Or, omit raisins and add 1 cup chopped dried apricots.
Makes 60 2-inch cookies

Old-Time Cinnamon Jumbles
Miriam Satz

Mix thoroughly:
½ **cup shortening (part butter)**
1 egg
1 cup sugar (or less)

Stir in:
¾ cup buttermilk
1 teaspoon vanilla

Sift together and stir in:
2 cups flour
½ teaspoon salt
½ teaspoon baking soda

Chill dough. Drop by rounded teaspoon about 2 inches apart on lightly greased baking sheet. Sprinkle with mixture of sugar and cinnamon (¼ cup sugar and ½ to 1 teaspoonful cinnamon). Bake until set, but not brown, at 375° for 8 to 10 minutes.

Famous Oatmeal Cookies
Miriam Satz
Madelyn's favorite

¾ cup shortening (¼ Mazola oil and ½ Crisco)
1 cup brown sugar
1 egg
1 teaspoon vanilla
1 teaspoon salt
1 teaspoon cinnamon
3 cups oats (quick or old-fashioned)
⅔ cup chocolate chips
½ cup sugar
¼ cup water
1 cup flour
½ teaspoon soda
½ cup chopped nuts

Beat shortening, sugars, egg, water, and vanilla together until creamy. Sift together flour, salt, soda, and cinnamon; add to creamed mixture; blend well. Stir in oats. Add chopped nuts and then chocolate chips. Mix well. Drop by teaspoonfuls onto greased cookie sheets. Bake in preheated moderate oven (350°) 12 to 15 minutes (don't over bake). For variety, add raisins or coconut.
Makes over 4 dozen cookies

Chocolate Chip Cookies
Miriam Satz

⅔ cup shortening (part butter or margarine)
½ cup sugar
½ cup brown sugar (packed)
1 egg
1 teaspoon vanilla
1½ cups flour
½ teaspoon soda
½ teaspoon salt
1 package (6-ounce) semi-sweet chocolate pieces
  (1 cup)

Heat oven to 375° (quick moderate). Mix shortening, sugars, egg, and vanilla thoroughly. Sift dry ingredients together; blend in. Mix in nuts and chocolate chips. Drop rounded teaspoonfuls of dough about 2" apart on ungreased baking sheet. Bake 8 to 10 minutes or until delicately browned. (Cookies should still be soft.) Cool slightly before removing from baking sheet.
Makes 4 to 5 dozen 2" cookies

Peanut Butter Balls
Miriam Satz

1 cup Karo syrup
1 cup peanut butter
raisins, chocolate chips, and chopped walnuts
1 cup sugar
4 to 5 cups Rice Krispies

Stir sugar and syrup and bring to a boil—boil about 5 minutes. Remove from heat. Stir in peanut butter, then raisins, chocolate chips, and walnuts. Add Rice Krispies and stir all with wooden spoon until completely coated. When cool enough to handle. Take small amount between palms of hands and roll into balls, and place onto margarine coated pan. Keep in tightly covered containers when cool.

Washboard Cookies
Miriam Satz

1 cup shortening (part Mazola oil)
2 cups brown sugar (or less)
2 eggs
1 teaspoon soda
¼ cup hot water or buttermilk
½ cup coconut
1 teaspoon vanilla
¼ teaspoon salt
4½ cups flour
1½ teaspoons baking powder

Cream shortening, add sugar and cream thoroughly. Add beaten eggs. Add soda to hot water and blend into creamed mixture. Add coconut and vanilla and mix well.

Sift flour, salt, and baking powder together and add to first mixture. Beat well. Form into balls the size of walnuts. Press each cookie lengthwise with tines of fork to resemble a washboard. Place one-inch apart on cookie sheet. Bake 8 to 10 minutes in 350° oven.

M and M Cookies
Miriam Satz

1 cup shortening (part Mazola oil)
½ cup sugar
2 teaspoons vanilla
1 teaspoon baking soda
1½ cups M & M plain chocolate candies
   (¾ pound bag)
1 cup brown sugar
2 eggs
2¼ cups flour
1 teaspoon salt

Cream shortening, sugars, eggs, and vanilla thoroughly. Sift together soda, four, and salt. Add dry ingredients gradually to creamed mixture mixing well. Stir in ½ cup M & M candies; reserve remaining candies for decorating. Drop by teaspoon on greased baking sheet. Decorate top of cookies with remaining candies. Use 350° oven and bake 10 to 12 minutes.

Recipes From Miriam Lerner Satz Family

Chili
Barry Satz

Soak 1 pound pinto beans overnight, drain. Add a little water and boil until done. Add 2 cans tomato soup, ½ onion, ½ green pepper, 1 pound browned ground beef (use 1 teaspoon olive oil). Season with salt and pepper. Add up to 1 tablespoon chili. Cook 1 hour. Add some corn (optional).

Noodle-Vegetable Cheese Casserole
Stephanie Cherniak

1 package (12 ounces) broad, ex-broad noodles
   or small shell macaroni or rotini pasta
corn flake crumbs
assorted fresh and steamed vegetables
1 cup shredded mozzarella or Cheddar cheese

Cook noodles or macaroni, add a small piece of butter or margarine, with a little corn flakes. Steam broccoli. Add fresh vegetables such as sliced carrots, zucchini, and peas or other vegetables. Mix together and add 1 cup shredded cheese. Sprinkle with corn flake crumbs. Bake in 350° oven for 35 minutes or longer.

Hamantaschen
Stephanie Cherniak

4 eggs
1¼ cup sugar
3 teaspoons baking powder
5½ cups flour (add a little after 5 cups until no
   longer sticky)
1 cup oil
2 teaspoons vanilla
½ teaspoon salt

Beat 4 eggs, add oil, sugar, vanilla, baking powder, and salt. Add flour gradually. Mix well. Roll on lightly floured board. Cut out circles with glass or cup.

   Place small amount of cherry or apple pie filling on circles and fold the dough over into a triangle, sealing the edges. Bake in 350° oven for 30 minutes or until light brown. Watch!

Applesauce
Stephen Cherniak

Twelve to fourteen Empire apples, peeled and cored. Slice in chunks and place in a 3-quart pot. Sprinkle top with 1 teaspoon brown sugar and cinnamon. Do not add water. Cover pot and cook on medium heat. Stir every 10 minutes and cook for 40 minutes.

Crispy Apple Crunch
Stephanie Cherniak

4 apples, peeled and sliced
¾ cup brown sugar
½ to 1 cup cooking oatmeal
½ cup melted margarine
1 cup flour
1 teaspoon cinnamon

Spread apples in 8" square pan. Mix all ingredients until crumbly and spread over apples. Bake in 350° oven for 30 minutes or until apples are soft. (Or can microwave on high 8–10 minutes until apples are tender.)

Baked Cranberry Sauce
Madelyn Satz

1 pound cranberries
1 cup chopped pecans
½ cup water
1 12-ounce jar orange marmalade
½ cup sugar (don't decrease)

Combine all ingredients. Spread in a 9 x 13 inch baking dish. Bake uncovered in a 350° oven about 30 minutes. Then transfer to a covered container. Store in the refrigerator. Serve warm or chilled over fruit or ice cream. Can be used as a meat accompaniment.

Stuffed Pasta Shells
Madelyn Satz

2 dozen large pasta shells
1 zucchini, unpeeled
 (yellow or green), diced
1 pound of low fat ricotta cheese
1 onion, diced
½ pound mushrooms, diced
1 clove garlic, pressed
½ bag spinach
½ pound grated mozzarella
½ pound shredded parmesan
1 large jar tomato sauce

Cook shells until pliable to work with. Cook fresh spinach, shredded slightly and drain well. Put some olive oil in skillet. Add 1 onion diced, a little dried red pepper flakes and 1 clove garlic minced.

Then add diced zucchini and mushrooms. Sauté for a few minutes. Combine all of the cheeses and mix in the spinach. Then combine with the rest of the ingredients.

Cover bottom of 13 x 9 inch pan with a generous amount of tomato sauce (Italian Spiced Chunky Tomato Sauce). Spoon mixture into shells so they are stuffed. Arrange shells on top of tomato sauce top side up. Cover entirely with sauce and sprinkle additional parmesan cheese on top. Bake in moderate oven 325-350° for 20 minutes or so until bubbly.

Carrot Cake
Madelyn Satz
Favorite dessert

⅓ cup boiling water
2 cups flour
1¼ cup sugar (or less)
1¼ teaspoons baking soda
1 teaspoon salt
1 teaspoon ground cloves (optional)
1 teaspoon vanilla
¼ to ½ cup raisins (golden)
2 cups finely shredded carrots (about 4 medium)
8 ounces crushed pineapple (drained)
1 teaspoon ground cinnamon
½ cup vegetable oil (canola)
3 eggs
½ cup chopped nuts

Do not let carrots stand. Heat oven to 350°. Grease and flour 9 x 13 pan. Beat carrots and remaining ingredients on low speed, scraping bowl constantly 1 minute. Beat on medium speed scraping bowl occasionally 2 minutes. Pour into pan. Bake until pick comes out clean, 45 to 50 minutes. Frost with Lemon Swirl Frosting.

Cream Cheese Swirl Frosting
Madelyn Satz

4 ounces low fat cream cheese
2 cups confectioners' sugar
¼ pound margarine
½ tablespoon vanilla

Mix all ingredients together. Spread frosting on cake and decorate with pecans.

Spicy Rhubarb Cake
Madelyn Satz

Follow Carrot Cake recipe but use 2 cups rhubarb (fresh or frozen) instead of carrots. Boil in ⅓ cup water, rinsed, drained, and chopped. Do not let rhubarb stand. Sugar 1¼ cups.

Spicy Zucchini Cake
Madelyn Satz

Follow Carrot Cake recipe but use diced zucchini (3 medium) instead of carrots or rhubarb. Do not let stand. Sugar 1¼ cups and ⅓ cup water.

Outdoor Grill Cooking

Hot Smoked Salmon
Michael Kojis
This recipe can only be prepared on a Weber or other kettle type charcoal grill.

Large fillet(s) of Atlantic, COHO, Alaskan, King, or other quality salmon (avoid silverbrite). The thicker, the better, 1/2 pound per person.
2 lemons
1 lime
fresh sweet basil
salt
smoking wood

Directions for preparation of smoking wood:
Start with about 1 pound of one of the following woods: cherry, apple, mesquite, or alder.

Somehow get it into chips/chunks between ¼" x ¼" 1" x 4". One can either enjoy the satisfaction of splitting oneself, or purchase prepared smoking wood from a quality barbecue retailer. In any case, do not use hickory, a common and popular wood, as it is only fit for red meats.

Soak in water for at least 1 hour. Drain ½ hour prior to use.

Thoroughly rinse, dry, and de-bone fillets. Marinate in solution of fresh lemon juice, lime juice, salt, and shreds of basil. (Small amounts can be used, then folded into a plastic bag for about 1 hour of soaking before grilling.) Minutes prior to grilling, massage with basil leaves, douse again with citrus juices, and salt.

Prepare grill (use own grill instructions).

Fill drip pan ¼" deep with water. Drop smoking wood directly on coals. Replace cooking grid.

Quickly crumple a wad of basil leaves an place on grid covering area the size of fillet(s). Place filet(s), skin side down, directly on basil leaves.

Cover and cook between 250°–300° for 15-25 minutes. After the first 5–10 minutes white globules may appear on surface of salmon. Remove by rinsing with juices and patting with absorbent paper towels. Halfway through cooking, rotate grid 180°. (Note: times and temperature ranges are quite broad, as they vary considerably depending upon ambient temperature, charcoal, ventilation settings/ thickness/moisture-content of salmon, etc. Generally, longer, cooler cooking is preferred.) Douse periodically with juices.

When surface browns, it's not done yet. Wait at least another 5 minutes, when it looks slightly overcooked and corners look like they're starting to burn, it's done. Douse again with juices.

Garnish with lemon/lime slices, capers, dried cherries, rosemary, parsley, or mint sprigs. Serve with rice, pasta, or couscous, a colorful mix of vegetables and whatever else strikes your fancy. *Absolutely a delicious dinner par excellence.*

SECTION III

Passover Recipes

Charoses
Miriam Satz

1 cup chopped apples
¼ cup chopped nuts
1 teaspoon sugar or honey
grated rind of 1/2 lemon
1 teaspoon cinnamon
2 tablespoons red wine (about)

Mix all ingredients. Add enough of the wine to bind the mixture.

Matzo Brie (Fried Matzo)
Miriam Satz

½ box Matzo broken in pieces
1 egg beaten or 1 egg beater
2 tablespoons olive oil or margarine
salt and pepper

Boil water. Cover broken pieces of matzo with the water, stir, cover, and drain immediately. Add beaten egg or egg beater, salt, and pepper. Use olive oil or margarine in large skillet. Fry matzo until crispy on bottom Turn over as much as you like until the matzo is crispy all over. Takes about 20 minutes.

Best Passover Popovers
Miriam Satz

1 cup water
⅓ cup shortening (peanut oil)
½ teaspoon salt
4 eggs
1 cup matzo meal

For shortening use vegetable or salad (peanut) oil, or margarine. Bring water and shortening to a boil. Then pour in meal and salt all at one time and continue cooking and stirring until the dough no longer sticks to sides of pan, a few seconds. Remove from flame and add unbeaten eggs 1 at a time, beating thoroughly after each addition. Drop by tablespoons on a lightly greased baking sheet or Teflon coated muffin pans.

Bake in hot oven, 450°, 25 minutes. Then reduce heat to 325° and bake 30 to 40 minutes or until browned. When cool, slit along 1 side. Insert about 1 tablespoon of filling or use as a bread roll. Great for school lunches by filling with slices of meat, tuna, or cheese. Can be used for dessert by filling puffs with preserves, stewed, dried fruits, or flavored, sweetened whipped cream. Nuts may be added to the filling.
Yield: about 12 puffs or 18 small ones

Egg Drops
Miriam Satz

2 eggs
¼ teaspoon salt
½ cup water
10 tablespoons cake meal or matzo meal

Combine well-beaten eggs with salt, water, and cake meal or matzo meal. Mix thoroughly until mixture is smooth. Drop by spoonfuls into boiling soup and cook 2 or 3 minutes.

Toasted Farfel for Soup
Miriam Satz
Martin's favorite

¾ box of farfel
1 or 2 eggs, beaten
1 teaspoon salt
2 tablespoons peanut oil

Combine and mix together all ingredients. Spread out in a flat baking pan. Separate the particles and brown in moderate oven, 350°, about 15 to 20 minutes. When cool, break into pieces. Especially good in chicken soup along with 1 or 2 matzo balls.

Variation:
For dairy, use as a breakfast cereal and add milk during Passover.

Best Matzo Balls
Miriam Satz

In order, combine:
3 eggs, beaten
1¼ cups cold water
¼ cup oil (peanut)
½ teaspoon garlic salt
1½ teaspoons salt
⅛ teaspoon pepper
2 cups Matzo meal

Mix above. Drop by spoonfuls into boiling water. Cook for 30 minutes. Serve in chicken soup.

Matzo Meal Coating for Roast Chicken
Marian Cabelly

½ **cup Matzo meal**
1 **cut up chicken**
salt to taste
garlic salt sparingly
pepper
seasoned salt

Put all ingredients into plastic bag and shake. Put pieces of chicken into bag and shake until chicken is covered with coating. Place in roasting pan, uncovered, and roast in 350° oven for about 1 hour.

Roast Chicken
Miriam Satz

1 **whole roasting chicken**
1 **carrot, sliced**
3 **quartered potatoes**
1 **clove garlic, chopped**
½ **cup chopped onion**
1 **stalk celery, sliced**
fresh parsley and dill

Place chopped onion and garlic in bottom of roasting pan. Add chicken and stuff with Passover Mushroom Stuffing. Add a little water. Bake uncovered in 325° roasting pan. Season with pepper and paprika. Baste occasionally. Can add carrot, celery, and potatoes when chicken is half-way done. Add chopped parsley and dill at this time. Cook about 2 hours or until chicken is done. Serve with Parsley-Pareve Potatoes if no potatoes are cooked with the chicken.

Passover Mushroom Stuffing
Maxine Arnow

½ **pound fresh mushrooms**
1 **medium onion, grated**
2 **tablespoons fat**
1 **teaspoon salt**
¼ **cup water**
2 **eggs, separated**
6 **tablespoons water**
6 **tablespoons Matzo meal**
1 **tablespoon chopped parsley**
1 **large potato, grated (optional)**
pinch of pepper

Slice mushrooms thin and simmer with grated onion, fat, salt, and ¼ cup water. Set aside to cool. Beat egg whites until stiff. Fold in yolks and 6 tablespoonfuls water. Gradually fold in Matzo meal, pepper, mushroom mixture, parsley (and grated potato, if desired). Fill cavity of 6 to 8 pound capon or chicken. Sew up and roast in 325° oven for about 2½ to 3 hours until browned.

Parsley Pareve Potatoes
Miriam Satz
Family favorite for holidays.

**6 to 8 small red potatoes or baking potatoes
  quartered**
2 to 4 tablespoons margarine (pareve)
fresh parsley, chopped
salt, pepper, and paprika

First, wash potatoes and peel once around the center and boil in salted water until done but not too soft. Let cool. Can be done ahead of time and stored in the refrigerator.

Second, sauté chopped fresh parsley in margarine and cook for around 5 minutes. Place potatoes in a baking dish and sprinkle cooked parsley over the top. Season with salt, pepper, and paprika. Bake uncovered in a 350° oven for at least one-half hour until browned.
Delicious!

Farfel Pancakes
Miriam Satz

Pour 1 cup water over 2 or more cups matzo farfel. Add 2 well-beaten eggs, 1 teaspoon salt and mix well. Fry on well-greased hot skillet. Serve with syrup, honey, or jam.
Serves 4 to 6

Matzo Meal Pancakes
Miriam Satz

½ cup Matzo meal
½ teaspoon salt
1 teaspoon sugar
3 eggs, separated
¾ cup water or milk

Mix dry ingredients. Beat egg yolks and add water. Combine the two mixtures. Let stand 15 minutes, then fold in stiffly beaten egg whites. Drop by spoonfuls on a well-greased griddle or skillet. Brown on 1 side. Turn and brown other side. Serve hot with syrup, jam, or sugar and cinnamon.
Serves 4 to 6

Passover Bagels
Miriam Satz

2 cups Matzo meal
pepper to taste
1 cup water
4 eggs
1 teaspoon salt
1 tablespoon sugar
½ cup oil (peanut)

Combine Matzo meal with salt and pepper. Bring water and oil to a boil. Add to Matzo meal mixture and mix well. Beat in eggs thoroughly, one at a time. Let stand 15 minutes. With oiled hands, roll into balls. Depress center and twirl until rounded. Bake in 375° oven for 50 minutes on greased cookie sheet until golden.

Matzo Charlotte (Passover)
Mary Gluchoff

4 Matzos
3 egg yolks
¼ cup orange juice
2 teaspoons grated orange rind
½ cup white raisins

1 medium apple (peeled and grated)
1 teaspoon salt
¾ cup sugar
3 tablespoons melted shortening
3 egg whites (stiffly beaten)

Soak Matzo in cold water for 5 minutes. Drain well and mash as fine as possible. Beat together egg yolks, orange juice and rind, raisins, apple, salt, sugar, and 2 tablespoonfuls shortening. Add Matzo and mix well. Fold in egg whites. Grease pan with remaining shortening. Bake in 350° oven for 30 minutes, until browned and set. Sprinkle with cinnamon and sugar.

Passover Matzo Pudding
Maxine Arnow

6 Matzos, broken up
½ cup sugar
¼ teaspoon cinnamon
2 apples, sliced
3 eggs, beaten
1 teaspoon salt
½ cup orange or pineapple juice
½ cup white or dark raisins
½ cup crushed pineapple
2 tablespoons peanut oil

Break the Matzos into small pieces. Put in colander and scald with boiling water. Drain well; add the rest of the ingredients and pour into a greased casserole. Bake about 1½ hours at 350° oven until nice and brown.

Matzo Meal Blintzes
Maxine Arnow

2 eggs
¾ teaspoon salt
1 cup water
½ cup cake meal

Beat the eggs and salt. Add the water and cake meal alternately. Melt enough fat in small skillet to cover the bottom. Pour in a thin layer of this batter. Fry golden brown on one side and turn out on a clean cloth. Stir the batter and continue frying in this manner until used up. Fill with cottage cheese mixed with egg and salt, or fill with jelly, chopped prunes, and nuts. Roll up, tucking in the ends, and fry in fat (peanut oil) until golden brown.

Matzo Meal Omelet
Miriam Satz

6 eggs
½ teaspoon salt
dash of pepper
¾ cup water
¾ cup matzo meal
3 tablespoons butter or margarine
preserves

Beat eggs until yolks and whites are combined. Add salt, pepper, water, and matzo meal. Heat butter or margarine in a large skillet; add egg mixture. Cook over low heat without stirring, lifting with spatula frequently to let uncooked eggs run underneath. When browned on bottom and firm throughout, make a 2" cut on either side of the omelet where it will be folded. Using broad spatula, gently fold in half; slide onto platter; serving immediately. Spread with preserves, if desired, before folding.
Serves 4 to 6
Good for a weekend brunch.

Best Passover Sponge Cake
Vivienne Arcus
Great Baker.

Use either 2 long narrow pans or 1 large tube cake pan. Separate 1 dozen eggs. Beat egg whites until stiff. To whites, add 2 cups sugar, the egg yolks, and juice of 1 lemon (or almond extract). Add ½ cup sifted cake meal and
½ cup potato starch. Do not overbeat.

Variation:
With the dry ingredients, you may fold in 1 cup finely chopped nuts.

Bake in a 325° oven until cake springs back when touched lightly with fingertip—about 50 to 60 minutes.
Best company dessert especially when putting fresh sliced strawberries on cut slices and topped with whipped cream.

SECTION IV

Sephardic (Spanish Jewish) Cooking

Meringues or Kisses

Miriam Satz
Good for Passover week.

4 egg whites
¼ teaspoon salt
1 cup chopped dates
1 cup sugar
1 teaspoon vanilla
1 cup chopped nuts

Beat egg whites and salt until stiff and dry. Beat in sugar gradually, sprinkling in 2 tablespoonfuls at a time. Add vanilla and continue beating until mixture holds its shape. Add chopped dates and chopped nuts. Shape in mounds with a spoon, pastry bag, or tube on greased cooky sheet covered with lightly greased heavy paper. Bake in very slow oven (250°) 50 to 60 minutes. Remove from paper while still warm.

Meringue Shells:
Shape in 3-inch mounds. Bake 1 to 1¼ hours. Remove from oven. Scoop out soft center with a spoon and place in oven to dry. To serve, fill center with ice cream or sweetened fruit, and top with whipped cream or dessert sauce.

Variations:
Fold in 1 cup shredded coconut before shaping or 1 cup finely pounded nut brittle.
Yield: about 30 large or 60 small meringues
Delicious! Great company dessert—pretty to look at.

Moussaka (Eastern Casserole)
Rose Bakish, Madelyn's Godmother

2 eggplants
2 eggs
corn flake crumbs
cooking oil
1 large onion
½ pound ground beef
salt and pepper to taste

Cut raw eggplant into rows ½ inch thick. Dip in eggs, then dip in corn flake crumbs. Fry in oil until lightly browned. While frying eggplant, sauté onion, ground beef, salt, and pepper in another pan. Place half of eggplant in greased casserole dish. Brush egg over this. Cover with ground beef mixture and top with remaining eggplant. Bake uncovered, in a 350° oven for 20 to 25 minutes. *Great dinner dish.*

Meat-Spinach Soufflé
Rose Bakish

1 pound spinach (frozen or fresh)
1 pound ground beef
2 eggs
pepper to taste
1 tablespoon matzo meal or bread crumbs
1 teaspoon salt
sesame seeds, if desired

Wash spinach thoroughly (if using fresh spinach). Cut as for salad; drain on paper towel to absorb water. Mix spinach with all ingredients except sesame seeds. Place in greased casserole dish; top with sesame seeds and bake for about 1 hour in 350° oven.

Variation:
You may form mixture into patties and broil.

Eggplant Pie
Louise Mitrani, Rose's sister-in-law

2 large eggplants (choose light in weight, as they have the least seeds)
1 pound ground beef (chuck)
2 slices stale white bread without crusts
2 eggs
1 teaspoon onion powder
½ teaspoon accent
salt and pepper to taste

Peel eggplants. Slice ⅓ inch thick. Dip in egg and fry until light golden brown. Line pie dish with half of eggplant slices. Salt slightly. Brown ground beef in dry pan until redness is gone, stirring constantly with a wooden spoon. Remove from fire. Sprinkle the salt, pepper, accent, and onion salt. Wet the bread slices thoroughly and squeeze out water. Add the wet bread and eggs to the meat and mash all with large fork until mixture is blended and creamy.

Put mixture on eggplant in pie dish, patting evenly with a spoon. Cover with rest of eggplant slices. Salt slightly. Bake, uncovered, in 350° oven for 30 to 40 minutes. Cut and serve like pie.

Variation:
The ground beef mixture can be used alone between pie crusts and baked in a 450° oven for ½ hour for a delicious meat pie.
Serves about 5

Zucchini Squash and Cheese Casserole
Louise Mitrani

2 zucchini (about 8 inches long and
    1½ inches in diameter)
3 eggs
½ cup ground Romano cheese or sharp cheddar
    cheese
¾ pound cottage cheese
1 small package cream cheese
2 tablespoons heaping matzo meal (no bread
    crumbs; they are salty and the cheese provides
    enough salt)

Peel zucchini. Grate on large side of grater. Take bunches between your hands and squeeze out all the water you can. Throw away the liquid. Mix thoroughly zucchini, cheeses, eggs, and matzo meal. Mash together with large fork. Grease casserole with salad oil. Add 2 tablespoonfuls oil to vegetable mixture, if you wish. Pour mixture into casserole and pat even. Bake, uncovered, in 350° oven for 1 hour or until it gets a nice light brown crust. Also, delicious cold and on sandwiches.
Serves 5

Spinach Pudding
Rose Bakish

1 pound spinach, chopped (frozen or fresh)
1 small box cottage cheese (8-ounce)
1 small package cream cheese (3-ounce)
2 to 3 eggs
pinch of salt
2 tablespoons (approx.) matzo meal
    (or 3 tablespoons bread crumbs)

Wash spinach thoroughly if using fresh spinach; cut as for salad; drain on paper towel to absorb water. Mix spinach with all the remaining ingredients. Grease casserole. Pour in spinach mixture, and top with grated Parmesan or Romano cheese. Bake for 35 to 40 minutes at 350°.

Eggplant Pudding
Rose Bakish

Use the same ingredients as in my spinach pudding, but substitute eggplant for spinach. Use 2 eggplants. Broil eggplant with skin on, in 450° oven for about 20 minutes until tender. Then dip in cold water, remove skin, and chop up insides, then proceed as for spinach pudding.

Celery Knobs
Rose Bakish

3 bunches celery
1 cup water
juice of lemon
¼ teaspoon salt
½ teaspoon sugar

Wash, peel, and slice celery. Combine all ingredients and simmer for 35 minutes in a covered pan. Serve with the juice either hot or cold.

Leeks
Rose Bakish

Wash leeks well and dice 2" in diameter. Add small amount of vegetable oil, lemon juice, a little sugar and a little water. Cover and cook on low flame until leeks are soft. Use as a salad and serve cold.

Leek Patties
Rose Bakish

Cut leeks 4 inches long. Boil about 20 to 30 minutes. Drain in colander. Squeeze water out when cool. Chop leeks, including cooked greens, well (like liver). Put some matzo meal, 2 eggs, less than ¼ pound raw ground beef. Mix all together. Make into patties and sauté in Mazola oil in a skillet. Use as a side dish.

Grape Vine Rolls
Rose Bakish

1 pound ground beef
¼ cup rice (uncooked)
½ teaspoon salt
¼ teaspoon black pepper
1 lemon
¼ cup water
1 can grape leaves
vegetable oil

Wash rice and mix with beef, salt, and pepper. Sauté for 2 minutes only in skillet with vegetable oil. Wash grape leaves carefully one by one. With the dull side of the leaf up, fill each leaf with 1 teaspoonful of the beef mixture. Fold and roll the leaf into a small roll. Arrange filled leaf rolls into rows in a pan. Squeeze juice from lemon over each row. Add ¼ cup water to pan. Cover and cook on low fire for about 20 minutes (until rice is cooked), adding water, if necessary to keep from burning. Sugar may be added to the sauce, if desired.

Spinach-Meat Patties
Rose Bakish

1 box frozen, chopped spinach, thawed
3 eggs
2 tablespoons bread crumbs
¼ pound chopped meat

Mix ingredients together and form into patties. Sauté patties in skillet until done.

Roasted Eggs
Louise Mitrani
Good for the High Holidays.

Cover eggs (1 dozen, more or less) with ice cold water and put on stove. Add a little salt. Start on low flame, boiling slowly. Put onion peels— skins—in water. Take some black pepper and 1 tablespoonful of oil. Make sure eggs are covered and cook at least 2 hours. Add hot water if needed to keep covered. Take out and dry with paper towels. Refrigerate until used. (The eggs have a nice brown color.)

Eggplant Appetizer
Heleen Greenwald

1 medium eggplant, peeled and cut into
  ½ inch cubes
1 medium onion, chopped
2 teaspoons salt
2 tablespoons olive oil
3 celery ribs, diced
3 ripe tomatoes peeled, coarsely chopped

2 tablespoons balsamic vinegar
1 teaspoon capers, strained (optional)
1 teaspoon salt
1 tablespoon pine nuts
1 bay leaf
⅓ cup chopped green olives
2 drops Tabasco (optional)

In a colander toss the eggplant cubes with 2 teaspoons salt. Let stand for 30 minutes. Rinse under running water. Drain and pat dry.

In a large frying pan, heat oil over medium heat. Add eggplant cubes and cook until they soften—about 4 to 5 minutes. Add onions and cook, stirring occasionally until softened—about 2 to 3 minutes. Add tomatoes, celery, pine nuts, and bay leaf. Reduce heat to low. Cover and cook 15 minutes.

Add vinegar, olives, capers, salt, and Tabasco. Cook 5 minutes. Discard bay leaf. Transfer to serving bowl. Serve at room temperature.

Cheesies
Rose Bakish
Popular Sephardic pastry

1 container cottage cheese (16-ounce)
2 eggs
1 package cream cheese (8-ounce)
½ cup bread crumbs
phyllo dough

Mix the ingredients together. Cover Phyllo Dough (bought in Greek stores) with a clean damp cloth, keep the dough moist otherwise it dies and crumbles and can't be used. Dough is already rolled out.

Take 1 plate and put some oil on it. Use hand or finger and dip in oil, then spread it on the dough.

Take dough and fold in two. Take 1 tablespoon of cottage cheese mixture and put on one corner and make a triangle—keep rolling. Oil stands on one side, mixture in another.

Grease 9 x 13 inch baking dish and arrange triangles not too close together. Brush cheesies with egg mixed with a little water. Brush on top and add sesame seeds. Bake in 350° oven for 25 minutes or longer.
Really great pastry.

Easy Lentil Soup
Rose Bakish

Soak 1 package of lentil beans overnight. Discard the water. Add as much water to cover as needed. Add 1 whole onion. Add a little Mazola oil. Later on add salt. (Can add sliced cooked frankfurters, if desired.) Cook for several hours until done. Freezes well.

Kohlrabi
Rose Bakish

Select leaves that are pale green and crisp, knobs about the size of a medium-size onion. One bunch serves 4 to 5. Trim off leaves, pare bulbs, and cut into ½-inch cubes. Cook, uncovered, in boiling salted water to cover, for 25 to 30 minutes. Drain, season with melted butter or margarine, and salt and pepper.

Green Tomatoes with Ground Beef
Rose Bakish

Cut green tomatoes in half and take out seeds. Fill with 1 pound of raw ground beef that has been mixed with 1 egg, a little cooked rice or bread crumbs. Sauté both sides of the green tomatoes in Mazola oil.

Add a little water to pan and cook covered for 10 minutes until everything is cooked well.
Good use of fresh green tomatoes at end of garden season.

Sour Cream Nut Cake
Rose Bakish
Everybody's favorite

½ **pound butter**
2 **eggs**
1 **teaspoon baking powder**
2 **cups regular flour**
1 **teaspoon baking soda**
1 **cup sour cream**
1 **cup sugar**
¼ **teaspoon salt**
1 **teaspoon vanilla**

Mixture for middle and top of cake:
1 **cup chopped nuts**
1 **teaspoon cinnamon**
½ **cup sugar**

Cream butter and add eggs, sour cream, and vanilla. Mix well or beat with spoon. Add dry ingredients after sifting together. It will form a thick batter. Pour batter (only half of it) over bottom of pan. Sprinkle half the nut mixture. Pour the rest of batter and sprinkle the remaining nut mix over top.

Bake at 350° for 45 minutes. Let it cool in the pan. Loosen with knife before removing.
Good Luck!

SECTION V

Favorite Recipes from Friends

Mixed Drinks and Appetizers

Champagne Punch
Tom Sturgeon

5 or 6 oranges, sliced very thin
1 cup fine, granulated sugar
2 bottles dry white wine (Moselle or Soave)
1 large block of ice
3 bottles of champagne, chilled

Place orange slices in bowl; sprinkle with sugar. Pour 1 bottle wine (Moselle) over fruit. Let stand 1 hour.

Pour this mixture over block of ice in a punch bowl. Add remaining wine and the champagne. May add club soda, if desired.

Champagne Punch #2
Connie Frohman

1 bottle champagne
1 or 2 large bottles of club soda
1 can frozen lemonade
2 teaspoons liquor (Cherry Herring)
1 bottle sauterne
thin slices of orange, lemons, and strawberries
1 quart lime sherbet

Mix the ingredients together and serve.

Cold Duck Punch
Harold Arnow

1 bottle Andre Champagne or other champagne
1 bottle Sparkling Burgundy
1 or 2 large bottles of 7-up
thin slices of oranges, lemons, and cherries

Mix the ingredients and add ice. Serve immediately.

Sea Breeze Drink
Patty Mosier

1 large can grapefruit juice, unsweetened
small amount of cranberry cocktail juice
add vodka to taste
use lots of ice

Southern Comfort Punch
Doc Ash

1 pint cranberry juice
1 can small concentrate limeade
1 can water
2 cans, small, Southern Comfort
ice, sliced oranges and cherries

Mix everything together and serve immediately.

Whiskey Sour
John Baird

1 can frozen lemonade
1 can water
1 can blended whiskey

Mix in blender. Add ice, cherries, and sliced oranges.

Cheese Straws
Mabel Ash

1 cup grated cheese—sharp cheddar cheese
1 cup flour
½ cup melted butter or margarine
½ cup scant water
1 teaspoon salt
pinch of red pepper

Mix together. Refrigerate overnight. Soft dough. Roll on floured board. Cut in strips, ½ inch wide, 4 to 6 inches length. Use a Teflon pan, no grease. Bake in 350° oven until tan or brown on bottom. Watch. Take and place on paper towels. Keep in tin on wax paper, uncovered.
Very tasty.

Chopped Liver Appetizer
Jean Reed

1 pound chicken livers
2 to 3 hard cooked eggs
1 tablespoon grated onion
2 to 3 tablespoons margarine
1 tablespoon mayonnaise
salt and pepper to taste

Clean and wash chicken livers thoroughly, removing any veins or gristle. Broil first. Then melt margarine in frying pan. Add livers and sauté until lightly browned and cooked through. Let cool.

In wooden bowl, chop livers until very fine (or may be put through a meat grinder). Grate hard cooked eggs and onion and add to chopped livers. Add any remaining margarine from frying pan and the mayonnaise and salt and pepper to taste. Mix until smooth. If too dry, you may add a bit more mayonnaise and melted margarine (parvu). Refrigerate mixture for 1 hour. Serve on a bed of lettuce. Garnish with radish roses, and serve with crisp fresh crackers and/or rye bread.

Sliced Cucumber Pickles
Sara and Eve Krauss

8 to 12 small fresh pickles, pricked with fork
1 gallon crock
2 to 3 teaspoons pickling spices
fresh dill
grape leaves
piece of celery (½ stalk)
3 or 4 cloves of garlic
½ cup coarse salt to a gallon of water
  (salt brine); add more salt, if desired

Place all ingredients in 1 gallon crock. Cover with grape leaves and place inverted plate on top. To sour fast, cut off ends of pickles. If not, prick each pickle several times. Check third day to see if more salt is needed. Check fourth and fifth day to see if pickles have soured enough. When done, place pickles in refrigerator. Freshen brine and add more cucumbers.

Easy Vegetable Dip
Connie Frohman

1 cup mayonnaise
1 tablespoon white horseradish
1 tablespoon yellow mustard

Mix together and refrigerate. Use on assorted cut vegetables (carrots, celery, green pepper, radishes, etc.)

Marinated Raw Mushrooms
Mary Sturgeon

½ pound fresh mushrooms
freshly ground black pepper
3 tablespoons wine vinegar or lemon juice
¼ teaspoon salt
½ teaspoon dried tarragon or oregano, crushed
½ cup olive oil

Cut the ends from the stems of the mushrooms and reserve for another use. Wash the mushrooms thoroughly, dry, and slice.

Mix remaining ingredients together, add to the mushrooms, and toss until all pieces are coated. Let stand at room temperature several hours. Serve with picks.

Fruit Dishes, Jell-O Molds, and Salads

Russian Fruit Salad
Esther Zabitz

Peel an pit 6 peaches. Slice apricots, strawberries, raspberries, and pineapple and add to peaches. Prepare a syrup of juice of 2 lemons, 2 oranges, 1 cup water, and ½ cup sugar, ½ teaspoonful of cinnamon, grated rind of lemon, 1 cup of red wine, and ½ cup of Madeira or rum. Boil this syrup for 5 minutes, then pour over the fruit, tossing the fruit, from time to time until cool. Place on ice and serve cold.

Scalloped Apples
Betty Gearinger

6 to 8 Macintosh apples
1 tablespoon butter
1 cup sugar
1 cup boiling water
½ teaspoon cinnamon or nutmeg
2 tablespoons cornstarch

Mix butter, spices, sugar, cornstarch, and water and boil together. When water comes to a boil, add red food coloring and pour over apples, (peel and quarter them first). Bake ½ hour, in a 375° oven. Get red hearts and sprinkle over the apples after they cool.

Frozen Cinnamon Apples
Connie Frohman

1 cup sugar
1 cup water
½ cup red cinnamon candies
8 to 12 medium apples

Combine sugar, water, and candies in saucepan. Cook over medium heat until candies are dissolved, stirring frequently. Simmer 5 minutes. Peel and core apples, and cut in halves. Cook a few at a time, in the syrup until just tender. Do not overcook and do not crowd apples in the syrup. Cool and freeze. To use, partially thaw. Use either as relish or salad, or garnish.

Garlic Crackers
Mary Wright
Dairy

Mix together in a large bowl 1 package of dry Hidden Valley Ranch Original, ¾ cup oil, 1 teaspoon garlic powder, ¾ teaspoon dill seed. Stir in a bag of oyster crackers (12- or 14-ounce)
A great snack.

Small "Duchess" Puffs
Helen Miller

½ cup butter or margarine
1 cup boiling water
3 or 4 eggs, unbeaten
⅛ teaspoon salt
1 cup sifted flour

Add butter and salt to boiling water. Stir over medium heat until mixture boils. Reduce heat and add flour all at one time. Beat vigorously until mixture leaves side of pan. Remove from heat and add 1 egg at a time beating thoroughly after each.

Use 1 teaspoon for each puff. Use 450° oven for 8 minutes, then turn down to 350° for 10 to 20 minutes. When cold cut open with knife and stuff with favorite fillings such as chicken, tuna, and egg salad.
Makes 4 dozen small puffs
This is a great appetizer.

Yum Yums
Mabel Ash

2 cups flour
½ pound butter or margarine
1 cup brown sugar
1 egg yolk, beaten
1 teaspoon baking powder
1 teaspoon vanilla
1 teaspoon cinnamon
1 egg white
½ cup ground nuts

Mix flour, butter as for pie crusts, add sugar, baking powder, cinnamon, and beaten egg yolk. Place on 1 large baking pan (9 x 13). Beat egg white and spread on top of mixture, sprinkle on nut meats. Have oven hot (350°) but turn down lower when putting in pan. Cut in squares while hot. *Delicious!*

Fruit Salad
Eleanor Shamis

2 cans whole cranberry sauce
16 ounces frozen whole strawberries, thawed
1 can (16-ounce to 20-ounce) drained crushed
   pineapple
½ cup chopped walnuts

Take frozen strawberries out of the refrigerator for an hour or two to be thawed before adding the other ingredients. When strawberries are thawed, add the rest of the ingredients. Stir and put in a bowl or mold.
Good when served with turkey.

Lime-Sour Cream Mold
Vivienne Arcus

2 packages lime gelatin
2 cups hot water
1 pint sour cream
1 (#2) can crushed pineapple, well drained
1 cup finely chopped nuts

Dissolve gelatin in hot water. Put in refrigerator until slightly thickened. Fold in pineapple, sour cream, and nuts. Put into mold and decorate with maraschino cherries.

Cottage Cheese Jell-O Mold
Mary Wright

1½ cups small curd cottage cheese
1 can Mandarin oranges, drained
1 medium can crushed pineapple
1 large box orange Jell-O
1 large cool whip

Mix powdered large box orange Jell-O with 1½ cups of cottage cheese. Add Mandarin oranges and pineapple, well drained. Use large cool whip. Fold in. Refrigerate. Cut into 3 x 3 inch squares and serve on lettuce.

Marinated Potato Salad
Lois Sturgeon
5 pounds potatoes cooked as usual

Combine:
⅔ cup corn oil
⅓ cup vinegar (cider)
2 tablespoons grated onion
2 teaspoons salt (or less)
¼ teaspoon pepper

Pare and slice potatoes. Toss with oil mixture while still warm. Marinate in refrigerator at least 2 hours. Add 2 cups chopped celery. Toss with 1½ cups salad dressing (use mayonnaise plus small amount vinegar and mustard). Chill. Serve on salad greens. Garnish with hard-cooked eggs.
Makes 17 servings
Great for covered dishes or picnics.

Crunchy Pea Salad
Mary Noll

1 package frozen (10-ounce) baby peas, thawed
1 cup diced celery
1 cup cauliflower florets
¼ cup dried green onions
1 cup cashew pieces
1 can (8-ounce) water chestnuts, chopped
½ cup sour cream
1 cup prepared Hidden Valley Ranch salad
   dressing

Combine all ingredients and chill before serving.

Cole Slaw
Lois Sturgeon

4 cups shredded cabbage
½ cup chopped green pepper

Sauce:
1 teaspoon salt
⅛ teaspoon pepper
2 tablespoons sugar
1 teaspoon celery seed
2 tablespoons vinegar (tarragon)
1 teaspoon prepared mustard
½ cup salad dressing or mayonnaise

Mix sauce ingredients until smooth. Combine with cabbage and green pepper. Refrigerate.

Soups and Vegetables

Black Bean Soup
Elisabeth Henrie

1 whole green pepper, chopped
2 or 3 cloves of garlic
1 onion
cooking oil

Sauté the green pepper, garlic, and onion in cooking oil. Cook 1 pound of dried black beans in 8 cups water. Boil for 3 minutes. Let stand for one hour. Add above mixture to soup, then add 1 16-ounce can of tomato paste and cook longer until done. (May add sliced frankfurters, if desired.)

Vegetable Soup
Cassie Selk

Take meat from shank bone and part of ground chuck. Cut small pieces of meat, sauté chuck. Add frozen package of vegetables. Add tomatoes, 4 cups water, and bay leaf. Add more water when necessary. Cook for hours.

Cabbage Borscht
Mary Gluchoff
Make a good, strong soup stock from beef and bones.

Add:
2 large cans tomatoes (packed in puree)
1 can beets (put through blender)
1 head cabbage, shredded
juice of 1½ lemons
1 tablespoon sugar
black pepper to taste

Cook until cabbage is tender. Adjust seasonings until taste is sweet and sour.

Lettuce Soup (with Peas)
Lois Sturgeon

½ cup parsley sprigs
2 cups consommé (parve) broth
1 can (#2) peas or 1 cup cooked frozen peas
salt and pepper to taste
½ head of Boston lettuce (maybe 2 cups of
**   garden lettuce) cut in pieces**
½ cup cream (optional)
croutons

Put parsley, lettuce, peas (undrained), plus ½ cup of the broth into electric blender. Puree at high speed—15 seconds.

Turn into saucepan, add remaining broth and simmer 5 minutes. Add cream and season to taste. Serve over plain croutons. (Good without cream.)

Vegetable Soup
Janet Stamm

Beef:
basic stock: leg portion, cross-cut for marrow. Cook long with salt; cut to small pieces when cooked. Use 2 quarts cold water or more.

Vegetables:
Corn, lima, and green beans, carrots, et al, especially tomatoes—may be fresh, stewed, or a can of soup. If fresh—as many as available in season. If frozen—your own or a bag of mixed vegetables from super-market.

Add:
Chopped onion, parsley, cabbage, and barley. Season to taste. Cook until done.

Potato Soup
Sonia Fisher

Cook potatoes separately, throw out the water. Cook onions and celery together until soft. Mix together and add milk, regular or skim. Season to taste. Add a little butter. Mash a few potatoes and put on bottom. Do not boil but simmer.

Vichyssoise Soup
Barbara Behr

1 can of potato soup
milk (1 can)

Heat. Place in blender and use chop, then cream.
Add seasonings and refrigerate. Serve cold.

Tomato Soup
Vivienne Arcus

1 whole can tomatoes or 1 quart cooked fresh
** tomatoes**
1 small can tomato sauce
2 sliced onions
5 tablespoons raw rice
salt, pepper, and sugar to taste
soup bones, meat or butter for dairy dish

Place 1 can whole tomatoes in blender. Put in pot
with 1 small can tomato sauce, 2 sliced onions,
salt, pepper, and sugar to taste. Add 5
tablespoonfuls raw rice. Add either soup bones or
lump of butter for dairy dish and 1 quart of water.
Cook about 2 hours.
*Refreshing summer dish when using fresh
tomatoes.*

Pickled Beets
Esther Zabitz

Cook beets, then peel and slice. Cook ½ cup white
vinegar, 1 cup or more water, add 3 tablespoons
sugar. Boil together. Add 1 slice of chopped onion.
Add beets. Let set 24 hours before eating.
Delicious!

Baked Onions
Editha Griffith

Peel desired amount of onions—medium.
Puncture center of each onion. Place in casserole
dish. Add 1-2 inches water. Dot with butter-salt-
pepper. Cover and bake in 350° oven for 1 hour.
Uncover and brown.

Creamed Onions
Editha Griffith

Cook (boil) onions. Drain. Add to medium sauce
(2 tablespoons flour and 1 cup milk).

Marinated Mixed Vegetables
Libby Rudnik

1 small head cauliflower, in florets
1 large package frozen lima beans,
** cooked 4 minutes**
3 carrots, cut in rings
1 large green pepper, cut in strips
½ pound green beans, cut in pieces
1 large zucchini cut in strips

Marinade:
3 cloves garlic, crushed
1 cup safflower oil
1¾ cups wine vinegar
⅓ cup sugar
2 teaspoons salt
2 teaspoons dry mustard
ground pepper to taste

Combine Marinade, pour over vegetables.
Marinate for at least 48 hours. Stir once or twice.
Serves 8

Braised Zucchini
Naomi Heskel

2 zucchini, washed and sliced
2 drops oil
4 drops soy sauce

Heat oil, add zucchini on high heat. Add soy sauce, stir about 5 minutes. Watch!

Beautiful Winter Vegetables
Lisa Mael

2 cups shredded carrots
2 cups shredded beets
2 cups shredded rutabagas (turnips)
¼ cup butter or margarine

Melt butter or margarine in a skillet. Toss in the vegetables and cover to steam for a few minutes. Uncover and stir briefly until tender, several minutes only.
A wholesome and tasty winter dish.

Marinated Carrots
Kathleen Hinkel

2 pounds carrots, cut lengthwise. Cook till tender crisp. Drain. Marinate overnight in:

1 cup chopped green pepper
½ cup chopped onion
1 cup tomato soup (condensed)
1 cup sugar
¼ cup vegetable oil
¾ cup vinegar (apple)
1 teaspoon salt
1 teaspoon dry mustard
1 teaspoon Worcestershire

Baked Squash
Susan Koff

Slice squash in half, unpeeled. Slice ¼ inch thick more or less. Put in baking pan. Cut peel off at edge. Sprinkle layers with a little brown sugar and cinnamon. Dot with butter. Cover and let stand awhile until beads of moisture accumulate. Add about ¼ cup water. Bake in 325° oven for 45 minutes. Cover while baking.

Pickled Cabbage
Sonia Fisher

1 large head cabbage, shredded
2 carrots, shredded
green pepper cut into small pieces

Sprinkle 1 teaspoon salt over the above ingredients. Let set for 1 hour.
   Boil ¾ cup sugar, ¼ cup cold water, 1 cup vinegar (white). After coming to a boil, cool a little bit. Squeeze cabbage to get juice out. To syrup mixture add 1 teaspoon mustard seed and 1 teaspoon celery seed. Mix the 2 together. Can freeze. Lasts 1½ weeks in the refrigerator.
Good for covered dish or picnics.

Poultry, Meat, and Fish

Oven Baked Chicken
Rose Bakish

One cut up chicken. Put 2 whole small onions in each corner of the pan. One carrot cut in big pieces. Cut 3 (2-inch) potatoes into slices. Arrange chicken over these vegetables. Add paprika on top. Cut 4 stalks celery. Cover chicken with the celery leaves. Put dill in between stalks. Add 1 cup cold water. Put parsley over top. Use no salt. Cover with aluminum foil. Bake in 350° oven for 2 hours. Then remove foil, and if not baked enough, add more water and cook for 15 to 30 minutes until done. Remove foil and keep in 350° oven for 5 or 10 minutes longer or close oven. Pour juice from foil over chicken.

California Chicken Divan
Molly Scarpino

3 pounds chicken filets, cut in chunks or regular breasts and legs
1 bottle Russian (Wishbone) dressing (8-ounce)
1 package Lipton's Onion soup
1 jar apricot preserves (10-ounce)

Mix all above ingredients. Place cut up chicken that has been skinned in Pyrex pan. Pour mixture over chicken. Bake uncovered in 350° oven for ½ hour and in 300° oven for ½ hour and check.
Delicious!

Microwave Coq Au Vin (Chicken)
Judie Hirshfield

1 medium onion (½ cup), chopped
2½–3½ pounds chicken (cut up or parts)
1 teaspoon paprika
½ teaspoon thyme
½ teaspoon salt (optional)
⅛ teaspoon black pepper
1 cup white wine
1 pound fresh mushrooms, quartered
2 teaspoons fresh parsley, snipped

In 3 quart microwaveable casserole, spread onion evenly. Arrange chicken around edges. Sprinkle with paprika, thyme, salt, and pepper. Pour in cup of white wine. Cover.

Cook on medium high (80% power) for 25–30 minutes. Add mushrooms and parsley. Cover. Cook on high (100% power) for 5 minutes.

Chicken or Beef Chow Mein
Ruth Schwimmer
For leftover meat.

Cook sliced onions and 2 cups diced celery in 1 tablespoon oil for 5 minutes. Add 2 cups each; diced chicken and/or beef and water, 3 tablespoonfuls soy sauce, 1 tablespoonful molasses.

Simmer covered for 15 minutes. Add 1 can drained bean sprouts or frozen spinach, shredded cabbage, or peas. Stir in 3 tablespoonfuls cornstarch blended with a little cold water. Cook until thickened. Serve on rice. Add Chow Mein noodles or Wheat Chex.

Curried Chicken
Connie Frohman
Chinese-style Gar Lay Gai

1 pound boned chicken
1 teaspoon cornstarch mixed with
  1 teaspoon water
1 to 4 tablespoons curry powder
1½ teaspoons salt
1 large onion
½ teaspoon sugar
dash of pepper
½ cup chicken stock

Slice chicken into uniform 1 inch pieces. Cut onion into half rings or lengthwise strips. Mix cornstarch solution and add sugar and pepper. Set beside pan. Note: use curry powder depending on your own preference. Start low; you can always add more.

Using a low flame, stir fry or brown curry powder and onion until odor of curry is pungent. Add chicken and stir, next add stock and salt and bring to high heat. Cover, cook until chicken is done, about 6 minutes, stirring occasionally. Stir in cornstarch mixture and mix until gravy thickens.
Serves 4

Stir-Fry Chicken in Wine Sauce
Marian Cabelly

Place skinned chicken breasts in 3" deep pan. In a big skillet put in some parvu Mazola margarine, chopped green onions, and green pepper. Sauté until clear, not brown. Throw in mushrooms, heat and toss them around until slightly done. Add 2½ cups cold water, 2 tablespoons Carmel Kosher soup mix. Use seasoned salt in water mixture. Add ¼ to ½ cup white wine. Mix in vegetables. Stir and

bring to a bubble and pour over chicken. Cover and let it all set for a couple of hours. Put in 350° or 375° oven. No cover. Add tin foil if getting dry. Bake for 1 hour.

Barbecued Chicken
Vivienne Arcus

1 cup tomato ketchup
½ teaspoon Tabasco sauce
2 tablespoons wine vinegar
1 teaspoon dry mustard
¼ cup oil
2 tablespoons brown sugar

Marinate chicken pieces overnight. Turn often. To bake: shake excess sauce from chicken parts. Place pieces on rack in shallow pan. Bake in 325° oven about 1½ hours. Baste every 15 minutes with sauce and turn often. Let final layer of sauce dry on chicken parts before removing from oven. This sauce is also delicious on chicken cooked over charcoal on grill. However, if cooked in this manner, it must be cooked slowly and thoroughly over coals. You may start the chicken in your oven, and finish it outdoors.
Yields about 1¼ cups

Chicken Breasts in Marsala Wine
Connie Frohman

Cover flattened breasts with flour. Place parve margarine and mushrooms in skillet. Pour Marsala wine and cook until boiling and thickened. Add chicken on top and cook until done—not too long.

Apricot Chicken Breasts
Peg Woznek

1½ cup orange juice
1 teaspoon lemon juice
15–20 dried apricots
2 tablespoons apricot brandy
2 tablespoons cornstarch
dash of ground cloves
4 boned, skinned chicken breasts (split)
3 tablespoons flour
¼ teaspoon salt
⅛ teaspoon pepper
2 tablespoons oil

Combine orange juice, lemon juice, and dried apricots in saucepan. Simmer to soften apricots slightly while browning chicken.

Combine flour, salt, and pepper in bag. Shake chicken in flour to coat lightly. Brown chicken in oil. Add apricot brandy to juice mixture. Combine cornstarch, a little water, and ground cloves and add to juice to thicken slightly. It will thicken more while baking.

Place chicken in casserole and pour orange juice apricot mixture over it. Cover lightly with foil. Bake in 350° oven for about 1 hour.
Attractive company dish and tasty as well.

Rib Roast of Beef
Dottie Halfmann

Roast should have at least 3 ribs. Take out of refrigerator 1 hour before roasting. Use 375° oven and roast beef 1 hour. (Four hours before eating—that is—baked at 10:00 A.M. and stopped at 11 A.M., can be reheated anytime after 3 pm.)

Do not open oven door. Place roast on bottom rack 45 minutes before serving—turn on oven after 45 minutes, let meat stand outside of oven for 10 minutes before serving.

Flanken (Short Ribs)
Rose Bakish

2 pounds flanken
4 stalks celery, sliced
1 cup water or more
2 medium onions, chopped
2 carrots—2 or 3 chunks
black pepper and garlic powder

Place meat in roasting pan or Dutch oven. Add vegetables and a little water. Cover. Takes a long time (2½ hours) on top of stove using low heat. Don't open pot. After an hour, add ½ glass of water. Take fat out before serving. Don't eat vegetables because of fat. Add black pepper. Serve with other vegetables.

Chinese Steak
Miriam Reisman

Combine and simmer 8 to 10 minutes, then allow to cool:

½ cup honey
½ cup consommé or broth
¼ cup soy sauce or Worcestershire sauce
  or combination
¼ teaspoon ginger
2 tablespoons catsup
dash of garlic

Meanwhile, sprinkle flank steak (or any other meat) lightly with tenderizer. Marinate in sauce; cover and refrigerate at least 15 hours. Broil or barbecue to desired doneness after removing from marinade. After meat is broiled, keep in oven with marinade poured over it. Carve diagonally into thin slices.

Chili
Monica Allen

Soak pinto beans in water overnight. Drain and cook until done. Brown 1 pound of lean ground beef in skillet. Add salt and pepper to taste. Add can of tomato paste and water to soupy consistency. Add sliced garlic, 1 teaspoon to 1 tablespoon of chili or more as desired. Cover pan and simmer for 1 hour. Add drained beans and simmer from 45 minutes to 1 hour, covered. Add water if necessary.

Boiled Tongue
Rose Bakish

1 beef tongue
1 onion, carrot, and celery
season with salt and pepper

Cook tongue in water to cover. Change water after it boils. Cover with water again and add whole onion, carrot, celery, and season with salt and pepper. Add fresh dill and parsley (optional). Cook 2 or 3 hours. Use low heat. When cooked, drain water and discard vegetables.

Peel tongue. Add cooking oil to pan and put in tongue. Cover and simmer for 20 minutes. To reheat, place sliced tongue in double boiler for 10 minutes.

Fried Liver in Sweet and Sour Sauce
Miriam Reisman

2 tablespoons flour
4 large thin slices of liver
1 egg, beaten 1 minute with fork
4 tablespoons bread crumbs
4 tablespoons parve margarine
1 tablespoon sugar
4 teaspoons lemon juice

Broil liver and slice about ¼ inch thick. Flour liver, dip in egg, and roll in bread crumbs. Melt 3 tablespoonfuls margarine in skillet, add liver and brown on both sides, allowing about 5 minutes a side.

Remove liver to serving dish. Add 1 tablespoonful margarine and sugar to skillet, and cook slowly until sugar is melted. Remove from fire; add lemon juice and mix well. Return liver to pan and turn in sauce until well covered on both sides. Serve immediately.
Serves 4

Potato Liver Knishes
Vivienne Arcus

6 potatoes
2 eggs
½ cup Matzo meal
2 large onions, diced
3 tablespoons oil
½ pound chicken livers
salt and pepper, to taste

Boil and mash potatoes; add eggs, matzo meal, salt, and pepper. Mix well. Broil liver first, then fry liver and onions in oil and chop together. Season. Take enough of the mashed potatoes in the palm of your hand to form a patty and flatten and shape. Place a small amount of the liver mixture in the center of each patty and fold potato over so the liver is in the middle. Flatten patty and fry in oil on both sides until golden brown.

Stuffed Cabbage
Mary Gluchoff

1 head cabbage (with large leaves)
1 pound chopped beef
1 tablespoon raw rice
¼ cup ice water
1 egg
1 medium onion, grated

Combine all ingredients except cabbage for meat filling

Sauce:
2 cans tomato sauce (medium size)
lemon juice, salt, pepper, and sugar to taste

Soften the cabbage in boiling water for about 5 minutes. Cut out core. Put 1 tablespoonful of meat filling in each cabbage leaf. Roll up and place in pot. Cover with tomato sauce seasoned to taste (sweet and sour) with salt, pepper, lemon juice, and sugar. Cook for about 1½ hours on top of stove with lid.

Beef and Rice Bake
Lois Sturgeon

Sauté:
1 cup chopped onion and celery in
**   2 tablespoons oil for 5 minutes.**

Add:
1 pound ground beef. Cook over low heat until
**   brown, breaking up meat as it cooks.**

Stir in:
1 to 1½ teaspoons salt
1 tablespoon sugar
1 teaspoon chili powder. Reserve.

Place 1 bay leaf in bottom of 2-quart bean pot or casserole. Spread ½ of meat mixture over bottom, cover with ¼ of rice (½ cup raw rice, total); repeat layers.

Pour over all:
2½ cups hot tomato juice plus
1 cup hot water

Bake, covered in 350° oven for 1½ to 2 hours, till rice is done. Stir with fork occasionally. If necessary, add hot water during baking.

Lasagna
Eleanor Shamis

½ onion, diced
2 garlic cloves, minced
  (or ¼ teaspoon garlic powder
1 or 2 cans mushrooms, diced

Sauté ingredients in 2 tablespoonfuls oil about 2–3 minutes.

Add:
2 12-ounce cans Contadina tomato paste
4 12-ounce cans water
1½ teaspoons oregano leaves
1½ bay leaf
½ teaspoon salt
¼ teaspoon pepper
1 pound ground round beef, cooked and drained

Let simmer about 2 hours uncovered or lightly covered.

One package lasagna pasta cooked according to directions. Can add teaspoon of oil in boiling, unsalted water. Drain and lay between plastic wrap—until ready to use.

Put some sauce in bottom of greased pan. (Use at least 2 pans.) Add 2 layers of lasagna. Add sauce over lasagna. Repeat, ending with sauce.

Bake about 30–45 minutes at 350°.

Barbecued Ground Beef
Rose Bakish

2 pounds ground beef
1 teaspoon salt
1 teaspoon mustard (regular)
1 tablespoon Worcestershire
1 onion, minced
1 teaspoon black pepper
1 teaspoon white vinegar
1 tablespoon sugar
1 bottle ketchup (8-ounce), rinse bottle and pour over meat

Sauté onion until soft. Add rest of ingredients. Cook for 2 hours on top of stove on low flame. Stir often. (Freezes nicely.)

Danish Meat Balls
Connie Frohman

2 slices white bread
1 cup cold water
1 pound chopped beef
1 small onion, minced
¾ teaspoon salt
¼ teaspoon pepper
¼ teaspoon nutmeg
1 egg
¼ cup warm water
4 tablespoons shortening
1 cup hot water
1 bay leaf
1 bouillon cube
flour

Soak bread in cold water. Squeeze dry, and crumble with fingers. Add meat, onion, seasonings, and egg; mix well. If needed, add enough water, gradually, to make a manageable mixture. Shape into balls, roll in flour and brown in heavy skillet in melted shortening. When all meat balls are browned, add 1 cup hot water, the bouillon cube and bay leaf. Cover pan and simmer ½ hour.

Quick and Easy Chop Suey
Jean Reed

1½ pounds ground beef
2 cans fancy Chop Suey vegetables
2 cups liquid reserved from above
4 tablespoons parve margarine
3 tablespoons flour
salt, pepper to taste
soy sauce to taste
1 can crisp Chinese noodles

Brown ground beef in skillet. Place Chop Suey vegetables in large pot, draining and saving 2 cups of the liquid. Add browned beef to the vegetables in the pot. In frying pan, melt margarine, stir in flour and then add the liquid from the vegetables. Season to taste with salt, pepper, and soy sauce. Cook until sauce thickens, stirring to keep smooth. Add this sauce to beef and vegetable mixture, and steam for 15 minutes. Serve over steamed rice and top with crisp Chinese noodles.

Frankfurters and Sauerkraut
Bob Reeder

1 large can sauerkraut
frankfurters
1 cup coffee

Drain and run water through sauerkraut. Cook on stove until most water has disappeared. Cook frankfurters (1 or more) separately. Add 1 cup coffee to sauerkraut. Slice frankfurters and add to the sauerkraut. Put in 325° oven for over 2 hours.

Chopped Meat Sauce for Spaghetti
Miriam Reisman

1½ pounds ground beef
1 tablespoon olive oil
1 clove garlic
½ medium onion, chopped
1 teaspoon chopped parsley
1 can tomatoes (medium)
2 small cans tomato puree
⅛ teaspoon salt
⅛ teaspoon pepper
½ teaspoon chopped basil
2 bay leaves
1 tablespoon parve margarine
1 4-ounce can mushrooms, stems and pieces or ¼ pound fresh mushrooms, cut in pieces

Place chopped meat, oil, garlic, onions, mushrooms, and parsley in saucepan and brown slowly, stirring frequently to prevent meat from cooking in lumps. Remove garlic as soon as browned. Add tomatoes, tomato puree, salt, pepper. Cover pan and simmer 1 hour. Add basil, bay leaves and cook 1 minute longer. Remove from fire and add margarine. Makes enough sauce for 1 pound spaghetti or other macaroni dishes.

Frankfurter and Bean Casserole
Vivienne Arcus

3 cans vegetarian baked beans
1 can tomato sauce
½ cup dark brown sugar
chopped onions and dry mustard (optional)
2 pounds Kosher franks (cut into 1/2 inch pieces)
salt and pepper to taste

Combine all ingredients. Bake, uncovered, for 1 to 1½ hours. Stir often.

Orange-Lemon Halibut Steaks
Marian Cabelly

2 halibut steaks
   (1½ pounds each and cut 1 inch thick)
¼ cup butter or margarine
2 tablespoons chopped green onion
2 tablespoons chopped parsley
2 tablespoons lemon juice
1 can frozen orange juice, thawed (6-ounce)
salt to taste

About 30 minutes before serving; in medium saucepan over medium heat melt butter or margarine and fry green onion and parsley until onion is tender. Stir in undiluted orange juice, lemon juice, and 1 teaspoonful salt (approx.) and cook until heated through.

Meanwhile, preheat broiler. Sprinkle halibut steaks with salt and brush with orange juice mixture. Place in broiler pan and broil 5 minutes. Turn steaks and brush with more orange juice mixture. Broil 5 minutes or until fish flakes easily when tested with fork. Serve with remaining orange juice.
Serves 6

Broiled Fish (Greek Style)
Judy Weinberg

3 whole fish (trout, porgy, any fatty fish)
2 teaspoons salt, ½ teaspoon pepper,
   ¼ teaspoon garlic powder, combined
2 large onions, in rings
2 large tomatoes, sliced
½ cup cooking oil

Make slits in skin of fish and rub in seasoning mixture of salt, pepper, and garlic powder. Place in baking dish. Place onions and tomatoes on fish.

Pour oil over ingredients in pan. Broil for 10 minutes on one side, turn and broil 10 minutes on other side.
Serves 6

Baked Fish Fillets Parmesan
Marian Cabelly

1 pound fish filet
2 tablespoons lemon juice
1 tablespoon butter or margarine
1 tablespoon flour
¼ teaspoon paprika
¼ teaspoon salt
¼ teaspoon pepper
¼ teaspoon nutmeg
1 can mushrooms (3-ounce)
¼ can grated Parmesan cheese

Heat oven to 350°. Place fish in greased baking dish. Sprinkle with lemon juice. In saucepan melt butter. Blend flour, nutmeg, paprika, salt, pepper, and enough milk to make ½ cup. Add this flour mixture to the melted butter, stirring until smooth and thickened. Pour over fish. Sprinkle with mushrooms and grated cheese. Bake uncovered 25 to 30 minutes. (Nutmeg and mushrooms may be omitted, if so desired.)

Casseroles–Noodles, Rice, Cheese, and Egg Dishes

Vegetable Casserole
Mary Noll

1 large tomato
1 cup cauliflower
1½ cups broccoli
1 medium turnip
1 medium zucchini
15 salted club crackers (Keebler or Ritz)
1½ teaspoons Worcestershire sauce
2 tablespoons dry white wine
1 teaspoon thyme
1 teaspoon basil
salt and pepper to taste
8 tablespoons butter
1 cup grated cheddar cheese

Break cauliflower and broccoli into florets. Seed and chop tomato. Peel and chop turnip into small chunks. Place turnip in boiling water for 5 minutes. Drain. Chop zucchini into bite size pieces. Toss together and place in casserole.

Melt 6 tablespoons butter. Add Worcestershire, wine, basil, thyme. Pour over veggies. Sprinkle with salt and pepper. Crush crackers and mix with remaining 2 tablespoons melted butter. Sprinkle over top, and bake 25 to 30 minutes in a 350° oven. Sprinkle with grated cheese and bake until melted—uncovered.

Fresh Bean Casserole
Lois Sturgeon

prepare 4 cups green and/or wax beans
chop 1–1½ onion
chop 1 green pepper

Butter a casserole dish. Put alternate layers of beans, onion, pepper, beginning and ending with beans. Sprinkle salt and paprika on each layer. Dot with butter or margarine.

Cover casserole and bake at 350° oven for 1 hour, or until beans are tender. If necessary, add small amount of hot water when half done. Cover with toast crumbs or croutons (au gratin).

Corn and Broccoli Casserole
Connie Frohman

1 package frozen, chopped broccoli
1 can cream style corn
1 egg, beaten
1 tablespoon grated onion
1 tablespoon melted butter or margarine
½ cup dry bread crumbs

Cook and drain broccoli. Combine with next 4 ingredients and ¼ cup of the bread crumbs. Place some bread crumbs on bottom of greased baking dish. Pour mixture into dish. Butter the remaining crumbs and sprinkle on top. Bake at 350° for 30 to 40 minutes.
Good covered dish for picnics.

Uncle Miltie's Potato Latkes
Esther Zabitz
Our latke king

4 small potatoes
1 egg
1 small grated onion
1 teaspoon salt
1 tablespoon flour

Grate potatoes or use food processor, add egg, salt, and flour. (Matzo meal may also be used in place of the flour.) Mix well and drop by spoonfuls to fry in oil. When done, place on paper to absorb some of the oil. *Enjoy!*

Boiled Bulgur
Naomi Heskel

1 cup bulgur
¼ teaspoon salt
2 cups tap water

Boil bulgar, water, and salt for 5 minutes over moderate heat. Reduce heat and cover and simmer for 15 minutes or until all water is absorbed. Remove from heat and allow to stand for 10 minutes before serving.

Dairy Kugel
Randy Krauss

½ pound medium noodles or whole package
4 eggs
½ pound butter (¼ stick)
lemon rind
6 ounces cream cheese
½ pint sour cream
1 cup sugar (or less)
½ cup white raisins
1 teaspoon vanilla
1 tablespoon lemon juice

Separate eggs—beat whites—boil noodles. Add butter to the noodles. Add sugar to yolks and cream well. Add sour cream and mix well, add cream cheese. Add all to noodles except whites. Then add raisins, vanilla, pinch of salt, lemon, fold in whites. Sprinkle top with sugar and cinnamon. Bake in 350° oven for 35 to 40 minutes.

Potato Noodles (Shlishkas)
Esther Falk

3 peeled potatoes
1 beaten egg
3 cups flour
½ teaspoon salt
2 tablespoons shortening
4 tablespoons butter or margarine
½ cup bread crumbs

Boil 3 peeled potatoes in salted water until tender. Drain, mash, allow to cool, and add 1 well beaten egg, 3 cups flour, ½ teaspoon salt, 2 tablespoons shortening. Knead a dough, and roll out to a ¼ inch thickness. Cut into ¼ inch strips, 2 inches long, and boil in 2 quarts salted water 10 minutes. Drain, and mix the noodles with 2 tablespoons butter or other shortening. Melt 2 tablespoons butter, add ½ cup bread crumbs, and mix thoroughly. Add to the noodles, and mix well. Sauté noodles in butter or margarine until lightly browned.
Great favorite among Esther's friends.

Tsimmes
Barbara Zabitz

1 cup orange juice or "Sunny Delight" an orange juice substitute
¼ cup brown sugar
4 to 6 sweet potatoes peeled and cut into large chunks
4 carrots, scraped and cut into large chunks
6 to 8 pitted prunes
1 teaspoon cinnamon
1 tablespoon margarine

Melt margarine in a heavy pot over low heat. Add rest of ingredients. Cook until done about 90 minutes.

Mrs. Kantor's Fabulous Noodle Kugel
Marian Cabelly

½ 16-ounce package Pennsylvania medium or broad egg noodles
1¼ cup (8-ounce) sour cream
¾ cup milk
½ cup seedless raisins
1 teaspoon vanilla extract
½ cup drained crushed pineapple
3 eggs
½ cup sugar
1 cup (8-ounce) cottage cheese
2 tablespoons butter or margarine

Preheat oven to 350°. Cook noodles according to package directions; drain. In large bowl, beat eggs and sugar; blend in sour cream, cottage cheese, milk, raisins, butter, pineapple, and vanilla. Add noodles and mix thoroughly. Turn into greased 2-quart baking dish and sprinkle, if desired, with cinnamon or crushed cornflakes. Or put 1 cup rice krispies or cornflakes, 1 teaspoon cinnamon in blender. Use chop. Spread lightly over top of Kugel. Bake 1 hour or until golden. Serve hot or cold topped with additional sour cream. Makes 6 to 8 servings.
Great for picnics.

Almond-Rice Stuffing or Casserole
Naomi Heskel

½ cup butter (or parve margarine)
1½ cups dry white wine
2 teaspoons salt
¼ teaspoon pepper
½ teaspoon dried thyme leaves
1 cup chopped blanched almonds
½ cup chopped onion
2 cups raw long-grain white rice
¼ teaspoon nutmeg
½ cup raisins

In hot margarine, in 6 quart Dutch oven, sauté onion, stirring until golden-about 5 minutes. Add wine and 3 cups water; bring to boiling. Add rice, salt, pepper, nutmeg, and thyme. Return to boiling; reduce heat, and simmer covered 20 to 25 minutes, or until liquid is absorbed. With fork stir in raisins and almonds. Cook completely before stuffing bird.
Makes 8 cups, enough for a 10-pound turkey
Great for Thanksgiving turkey.

Rice Cakes
Connie Frohman

½ cup rice
1 pint milk
3 eggs
½ teaspoon cinnamon
½ teaspoon nutmeg
½ cup sugar

Cook rice in milk 30 minutes or until tender. Mash with fork and cool. Beat eggs well, and add to rice. Stir in spices and sugar; mix well. Fry on one side on greased griddle until delicately browned. Turn carefully and brown other side. Serve with jam or syrup.

Rice Pudding
Cassie Selk
No eggs.

1 quart milk
½ cup raisins
sugar to taste
½ cup raw rice
little salt
nutmeg

Mix all ingredients and place in casserole dish, uncovered. Bake in 350° oven for over an hour until most milk has evaporated. Serve either warm or cold, as a side vegetable dish or as a dessert. Delicious either way.

Chinese Fried Rice
Judy Weinberg

1 large onion, diced
1 green pepper, diced
1 stalk celery, sliced thin
1 tablespoon sugar
5 tablespoons cooking oil
1 beaten egg
¼ cup cooked rice
1 can bean sprouts
1 small can mushrooms

Sauté onions, pepper, and celery in cooking oil until soft. Add sugar, stir and then add beaten egg, and cooked rice (if desired, add soy sauce at this time.) Cook, stirring for 5 minutes. Add bean sprouts and cook a few minutes longer. Serve over Chinese noodles.

Spinach and Rice
Mattie Hasson

1 package frozen chopped spinach
¼ cup uncooked rice
3 tablespoons cooking oil
salt and pepper to taste
juice of ½ lemon

Place all ingredients in saucepan. Cook over medium heat until water disappears and rice is cooked. Mix all together when cooked.

Noodle Rice Pilaf
Marian Cabelly

2 tablespoons butter or margarine
1 small onion, minced
1 clove garlic, minced
1 cup raw rice
2½ cups water
1 envelope Goodman's Noodleman noodle soup mix
2 tablespoons chopped parsley
freshly ground black pepper

Melt butter in saucepan; sauté onion and garlic for 3 minutes or until onion is transparent, but not brown. Stir in rice and cook, stirring for 1 minute. Add water and bring to a boil. Stir in soup mix, cover tightly, and cook over low heat for 30 minutes without stirring. Cover after adding parsley and pepper. Remove cover after a few minutes and toss with a fork.
Serves 4

Blintzes
Esther Zabitz

2 eggs
2 tablespoons salad oil
1¾ cup milk
½ teaspoon salt
6 tablespoons butter
1 cup flour

Beat the egg, oil, and milk together in a large bowl. Add the flour and salt; beat until very smooth. Chill for 30 minutes. The batter should be the consistency of heavy cream. If the mixture is too thick, add a small amount of milk. Melt 1 teaspoonful of the butter in a 7 inch frying pan. Pour 1 tablespoon of the batter into it, turning the pan quickly so batter will cover bottom. Fry until browned on one side only.

Filling (Cheese):
¼ pound cream cheese
¼ pound cottage cheese
1 teaspoon vanilla extract
2 egg yolks
2 tablespoons sugar

Beat all ingredients together until smooth. Place small amount of filling in blintz and fold. Fry or bake in greased pan until done.

Variation Filling: Blueberry:
2 cups blueberries
2 tablespoons sugar
2 tablespoons flour

Sprinkle blueberries with sugar and flour.

Quiche Lorraine
Susan Koff

Pastry for 2 pie shells:
2 cups flour
⅔ cup Crisco
1 teaspoon salt
4 to 6 tablespoons cold water
Or unbaked 9" pie shell (or 10")

Filling:
¼ cup bacos
1¼ cups grated Swiss cheese
3 eggs, beaten
½ teaspoon salt
1 medium chopped onion
¼ cup grated Parmesan cheese
1½ cups light cream
¼ teaspoon pepper

Cook onion gently until tender but not browned in 1 tablespoonful butter. Place bacos, onion, and cheese in unbaked pie shell. Blend together eggs, cream, salt, and pepper. Pour over mixture in pie shell.

Bake in moderate oven (375°) until mixture is firm and lightly browned, about 45 minutes. *Very delicious.*

Eleanor Deutsh's Cheese Pit
Esther Zabitz

cut crusts from 5 slices of bread and butter
¾ pound cheese, grated
4 eggs, beaten slightly
2 cups milk
½ teaspoon dry mustard
½ teaspoon salt
dash cayenne

Cut buttered bread into small cubes. Alternate layers of bread and cheese in a buttered baking dish. Mix all other ingredients together and pour over cheese and bread. Let stand several hours or overnight before baking. Bake at 350° for 1 hour.

Amish Funnel Cakes
Ruth Schwimmer

2 eggs, well beaten
3 tablespoons sour cream
2 cups milk (scant)
½ teaspoon soda
1 teaspoon baking powder
½ teaspoon salt
3 cups flour

Measure sour cream into a cup, fill cup with milk. Stir into beaten eggs. Mix flour, soda, baking powder, and salt. Add milk if batter is not runny. Heat deep fat until bread cube browns (375°). Pour 3 tablespoonfuls batter from pitcher into funnel holding finger over funnel spout. Remove finger, swirl funnel so batter forms a concentric circle 3 to 6 inches in diameter, starting from center. Drain, sprinkle with powdered sugar.

One Eyed Pete
Jean Reed
Breakfast fun

1 egg (whole)
1 slice white sandwich bread
butter or margarine

Melt butter in frying pan. Cut hole size of half dollar in center of bread. Place bread in frying pan. Drop whole, unbroken egg into hole in bread. Cook until bottom is set. Turn and cook other side. Continue to add butter as needed to frying pan to prevent burning.

Baked Cheese and Egg Dish
Betsy Marateck

8 eggs
1 cup shredded cheese (cheddar or mozzarella)
dash of salt
1 cup milk
1 small to medium onion, minced

Sauté onion in butter or margarine. Mix eggs, milk, and salt. Stir in onion and cheese. Pour mixture into greased 9 x 9 inch pan or 9 x 13 inch pan depending how many eggs are used. Bake in 325° oven for 40 to 45 minutes. (Half recipe is fine for smaller families.)

Paper Thin Pancakes
Jean Reed

1 cup flour
1 teaspoon baking powder
1 teaspoon sugar
¼ teaspoon salt
1 egg
1⅓ cups milk
butter or margarine (for frying)

Sift flour, baking powder, sugar, and salt together. Beat egg with fork. Add milk to egg. Add this liquid to the flour mixture, stirring until it is smooth. Add 1 teaspoonful melted butter for extra flavor. Heat margarine in frying pan until pan is very hot. Drop 1 tablespoonful pancake batter into frying pan for each pancake, being careful not to touch other pancakes in pan. Fry one side until bubbles form and edges become crisp. Turn and brown other side. Keep pancakes warm in oven until ready to serve. Serve with butter and syrup or jam.

Non-Fat Egg Rolls
Judith Brandt

1 package Egg Roll wrappers
1 red bell pepper, finely chopped
1 green bell pepper, finely chopped
2 cups broccoli, finely chopped
1 package (10 ounces) white mushrooms, finely
  chopped
1 package shiitake mushrooms, finely chopped
2 tablespoons teriyaki sauce (or Tamair soy
  sauce) plus 1 tablespoon brown sugar
1 clove garlic
1 teaspoon finely chopped fresh ginger

Using pan spray, sauté all vegetables until
tender/crisp. Add teriyaki sauce. Simmer 3
minutes. Drain.

Using egg roll wrappers, fill with vegetable
mixture (approx. 2 tablespoonfuls each). Fold
wrappers, using a paste made from flour and water
to seal wrappers.

Brown until crisp in heavy frying pan, using
no-stick spray. Serve with Duk sauce.

Breads, Coffee Cakes, and Muffins

Crane Pumpkin Bread (2 Loaves)
Cassie Selk

2 9 x 5 x 2 inch pans
1 cup corn oil
4 eggs, beaten
½ teaspoon cloves
2 teaspoons baking soda
⅔ cup cold water
2 cups pumpkin
3½ cups flour
1½ teaspoons salt
1 teaspoon nutmeg
½ teaspoon ginger
2 cups sugar
1 cup raisins
1 cup chopped nuts (pecans)
1 teaspoon cinnamon

Grease and flour 2 loaf pans. Mix corn oil, eggs,
water, and pumpkin. Add flour, salt, nutmeg,
cinnamon, baking soda, and sugar. Mix well. Add
raisins and nuts. Bake for 1 hour or 1 hour and 15
minutes in 350° oven.

Challah Sabbath Twists
Naomi Heskel

1½ packages active dry yeast
1½ cups lukewarm water
3 tablespoons corn oil
3 large eggs at room temperature
5–5½ cups flour
1 tablespoon sugar
½ cup honey
2 teaspoons salt
1 egg yolk
1 egg yolk with 1 tablespoon water for glaze

Dissolve yeast and sugar in one-third cup water. Set aside to proof in a warm place, about 5 minutes.

Mix the rest of the water and honey together in a large bowl. Stir in the corn oil, salt, and yeast mixture. Beat in the eggs and egg yolk.

Using a wooden spoon, stir in 3 cups of flour and beat until well blended. Begin adding the remaining flour.

Turn dough out onto well-floured board and knead for 10 minutes. Add additional flour while kneading to make a dough that is smooth.

Place dough in an oiled bowl, turn the ball of dough in the bowl to oil all sides, cover with clean tea towel and set aside until doubled in bulk, about 1 hour.

Punch down and knead for a minute or two. Divide dough in six rolls. Take three long rolls and braid, set that on a foil-lined cookie sheet. Braid last three long rolls, place on foiled cookie sheet. Let rise about 45 minutes.

Preheat oven to 400°. Sprinkle poppy seeds on top of egg wash, if desired. Gently brush bread with egg wash. Place in center of oven and bake for 40 minutes.

Processor Orange Bread
Connie Frohman

2½ cups flour
1 teaspoon salt
2 tablespoons sugar
3 tablespoons margarine cut up
1 package yeast
¼ cup warm water
1 tablespoon sugar
⅔ cup orange juice

Combine first 4 ingredients in processor. Process 20 seconds. Proof yeast with water and 1 tablespoonful sugar. Add to flour and process 5 seconds. With motor running, add ⅓ cup orange juice and add enough more juice just until mixture forms a ball on top of the blades. Knead on floured surface a few times, till smooth.

Place in greased bowl, turn to grease top. Cover-let rise till double, about 1½ hours. Punch down, roll out to a rectangle. Wet surface with water, sprinkle with cinnamon sugar and raisins. Roll tightly, seal ends. Put in greased loaf pan. Cover and let rise till double about 1 hour. Bake at 375° for 30 minutes.

Pumpkin Bread
Fay Hollister

1 regular loaf pan
1⅔ cups flour
1 teaspoon baking soda
½ teaspoon cinnamon
⅓ cup shortening (Crisco)
½ teaspoon vanilla
1 cup mashed pumpkin
½ cup chopped walnuts or pecans
¼ teaspoon baking powder
¾ teaspoon salt
½ teaspoon nutmeg
1⅓ cups sugar
2 eggs
¼ cup cold water

Grease and flour pan. Sift dry ingredients together. Cream shortening, sugar, and vanilla together. Add eggs, one at a time. Stir in pumpkin and flour in four additions with water. Add nuts. Bake in 350° oven for 45 to 55 minutes.

Rhubarb Crunch Coffee Cake
Liz Kinslinger

½ cup plus 2 tablespoons margarine
2 eggs
1 teaspoon vanilla
¾ cup sour cream
1¾ cups finely chopped rhubarb
1 teaspoon cinnamon
¼ cup chopped nuts
1 cup light brown sugar (dark okay)
1 teaspoon baking soda
2 cups sifted flour
½ cup chopped nuts
½ cup granulated sugar
½ teaspoon nutmeg

Cream ½ cup margarine and brown sugar. Blend in eggs and vanilla. Mix soda in sour cream. Stir in alternately with flour. Add ½ cup nuts, rhubarb. Put in lightly greased and floured 13 x 9 inch pan.

Combine remaining 2 tablespoonfuls margarine, sugar, cinnamon, nutmeg, and 1/4 cup nuts. Sprinkle over batter. Bake in 350° oven about 40 minutes.

Egg Kichlech
Mary Gluchoff

2 eggs
1¼ cup flour
½ teaspoon salt
½ teaspoon baking powder

Knead well all the ingredients. Roll out dough at least ½ inch thick. Sprinkle with sugar. Prick all over with fork. Cut diagonally into diamonds, each side to be about 3 inches long. Sprinkle pan with flour before putting in the kichlech. Bake in moderate oven about one-half hour until brown.

Mohn (Poppy Seed) Shortbread
Vivienne Arcus

Knead by hand:
½ pound butter
1 cup sugar
2 cups flour
1 teaspoon cinnamon
1 teaspoon vanilla
1 egg yolk

Grease cookie sheet with lip all around. Flatten dough with fingers. Brush with egg white and sprinkle generously with poppy seeds. Bake 30 to 35 minutes in 350° oven. Cut into squares while hot.

Never-Fail Challah
Lisa Mael

2 tablespoons yeast
2 cups warm water
2 to 3 eggs
¼ to ½ cup honey or sugar
2 teaspoons salt
2 tablespoons to ⅓ cup butter or oil
7 to 8 cups regular white or unbleached white flour

Egg wash:
optional: sesame or poppy seeds

Dissolve yeast in water. Add eggs, honey, salt, butter or oil, and about 3½ cups flour. Beat well by hand or with electric mixer. Add remaining flour to make a soft dough. Knead 5 to 10 minutes, adding more flour if necessary. Use as little flour as possible for a delicate Challah. It should be velvety soft. Let rise until double 1½ to 2 hours. Punch down and let rise again, if desired.

Shape into 2 twisted or braided loaves; place on greased cookie sheets and let rise until doubled. Brush with egg wash and sprinkle with seeds, if desired.

Bake at 350° to 375° for 30 to 45 minutes, until golden brown. Serve warm or cool. (A round braided loaf for the High Holidays can be baked in a greased cake pan. Use vegetable spray.) Hearty appetite!

Chocolate Chip Coffee Cake
Lois Sturgeon

Cream together:
½ cup margarine
1 cup sugar
2 eggs

Add:
2 cups sifted flour
1½ teaspoons baking powder
1 teaspoon baking soda
1 cup sour cream
1 teaspoon vanilla

Spread ½ of batter in greased 9 x 12 inch pan. Sprinkle ½ of topping over it. Spread rest of batter over this, sprinkle remaining topping on.

Topping:
½ cup sugar
1–1½ teaspoons cinnamon
6 ounces chocolate chips

Bake in 350° oven for 20 to 25 minutes.

Banana Muffins
Anonymous

3 ripe bananas
2 eggs
1 teaspoon vanilla
¾ cup light brown sugar
2 cups flour
1 teaspoon baking powder
1 teaspoon baking soda
¼ cup chocolate chips
1 stick margarine

Melt margarine. Beat eggs. Sift dry ingredients. Mix mashed bananas, sugar, and vanilla. Add margarine, eggs, and flour mixture Add chocolate chips. (Top with crushed nuts, optional). Use muffin pan and place paper cups on bottom, Drop 1 tablespoonful of batter into cup cake pan. Bake in 350° oven for 16 to 18 minutes.
Makes about 1½ dozen muffins

Desserts and Pies

Bread Pudding
Libby Rudnik

½ cup raisins
2 cups milk
¼ cup butter or margarine
3 cups white bread cubes
½ teaspoon cinnamon
⅛ teaspoon salt
2 eggs
¼ cup sugar

Soak raisins 20 minutes. Drain, heat milk and butter. Combine next 6 ingredients and raisins. Add milk. Pour into quart baking dish. Place dish in pan of hot water. Bake 350° for 45 to 55 minutes or until inserted knife comes out clean.

Lemon Curd Squares
Nina Feldser

Preheat oven to 350°. Sift together:
1 cup sifted flour
½ cup confectioners' sugar

Add and combine:
½ cup melted butter

Press the mixture into an 8 x 8 inch greased baking pan and bake 20 minutes. Meanwhile combine:

1 cup sugar
½ teaspoon baking powder
2 slightly beaten eggs
2 tablespoons lemon juice
2 teaspoons grated lemon peel
½ cup flaked coconut

Pour these ingredients over the baked warm crust and bake 25 minutes. Chill. Before serving, cut into 2-inch squares and sprinkle with confectioners' sugar.

Orange Sherbet Dessert
Katherine Nagel

1 large package orange Jell-O. Add 2 cups boiling water. Chill until soft. Add 1 quart of orange sherbet. Stir to mix. Add 2 small cans (11-ounce) drained mandarin oranges and 3–4 sliced bananas. Fold in 1 cup of whipped cream. Chill.

Pineapple Dessert
Rose Bakish
Stephanie's favorite

½ **cup butter or margarine**
2 **egg yolks**
½ **teaspoon fresh lemon juice**
1 **cup sour cream**
2 **egg whites, beaten stiff**
1½ **cup confectioners' sugar**
1 **can crushed pineapple (8¾-ounce)**
   drained well
Lady Fingers (2 packages)

Cream butter and sugar. Add egg yolks, lemon juice, and pineapple. Fold in sour cream and egg whites.

   Line pan with Lady Fingers (open flat) and spread half of mixture over them. Put another layer of Lady Fingers on top and add rest of mixture. Refrigerate 8 hours. Cut and serve.
Delicious dessert for company.

Strawberries Romanoff
Billie Henrie

3 **pints strawberries**
½ **cup white rum or kirsche**
vanilla
⅓ **cup sugar**
1 **large cool whip**

Marinate strawberries in refrigerator for several hours. Add cool whip later. Serve in sherbet glasses.

Fresh Peach Sauce
Mary Wright

5 **medium peaches mashed with fork**
½ **cup sugar (or less)**
½ **cup orange juice**
2 **tablespoons lemon juice**
1 **teaspoon vanilla**

Combine all ingredients in saucepan. Stir over high heat until boiling. Turn down heat and cook on simmer for about 15 minutes.

   Spoon over frozen yogurt or ice cream.
Great summer dessert.

Fruit or Lemon Squares
Deborah Poplawsky

Crust:
3 **cups flour**
¾ **pound margarine**
3 **tablespoons sugar**
1 **teaspoon salt**

Cream Mixture:
1 **16-ounce package cream cheese**
1 **16-ounce cool whip**
1 **cup confectioner's sugar**

Cream flour, margarine, sugar, and salt. Mix well. Spread on 10 x 16 x 2 cookie sheet. Bake in 350° oven for 10 to 15 minutes until light brown. Cool. Mix cream cheese with sugar until soft. Add cool whip. Mix well. Spread over crust.

Topping:
Spread 1 can of canned fruit pie or lemon pie filling. Place in refrigerator for 1 hour. Cut in 1 inch squares.
Pretty to look at and delicious.

Apple Crisp
Eleanor Shamis

**6 apples peeled and cut into chunks
and put in 8 x 8 inch baking dish
1 cup flour
1 teaspoon baking powder
½ cup sugar
1 egg**

Mix last 4 ingredients together. Spread over apples and sprinkle with cinnamon. Melt ½ stick of butter or margarine and pour over top. Bake in 375° oven for about 45 minutes.

Peanut Butter Candy
Almus Russell

**1 cup powdered milk
1 cup light Karo syrup
½ cup chopped walnuts
1 cup peanut butter
1 cup confectioners' sugar**

Mix all ingredients with a big wooden spoon. Put mixture on a plate. Mark in squares. Place in refrigerator for a couple of hours or deep freeze for 15 minutes. Then place candy in a bag of confectioners' sugar. Keep in refrigerator.

Perfect Pie Crust
Cassie Selk

**4 cups unsifted flour
2 teaspoons salt
1 tablespoon white or cider vinegar
½ cup water
1 tablespoon sugar
1¾ cups solid vegetable shortening (Crisco)
1 large egg**

Put flour, sugar, and salt in large bowl. Add shortening. In small bowl, beat vinegar, water, and egg. Add egg mixture to flour and mix well.

Divide dough into 5 sections and chill for one-half hour. (Divided dough may be wrapped in aluminum foil and frozen until needed.)
Makes 5 crusts

Lemon Sponge Pie
Betty Gearinger

**1½ cups sugar
4 eggs
¼ cup flour
1 cup milk
6 tablespoons butter
juice and rind of 1 large lemon
4 stiffly beaten egg whites**

Cream sugar, butter, and egg yolks. Add lemon juice and rind, flour and milk. Fold in egg whites last. Pour mixture on unbaked pie crust in a 10 inch pie pan. Bake for 45 minutes at 325°.

Crazy Crust Apple Pie
Elisabeth Henrie

**1 cup flour
1 teaspoon baking powder
¾ cup water
1 egg
2 tablespoons sugar
½ teaspoon salt
⅔ cup solid vegetable shortening**

Filling:
1 can (1 pound 5-ounce) apple pie filing or stewed apples
1 tablespoon lemon juice
½ teaspoon apple pie spice or cinnamon

Combine all ingredients for filling in mixing bowl.

No need to sift flour, measure by lightly spooning into cup and leveling off. In small mixing bowl, combine flour, sugar, baking powder, salt, water, shortening, and egg. Blend well at lowest speed. Beat 2 minutes at medium speed. Spread batter in 10-inch or 9-inch deep dish pie pan. Carefully spoon into center of bottom. Do not stir. Bake at 425° for 40 to 45 minutes until crust is golden brown.

Delicious Pastry for Pie
Vivienne Arcus

1½ cups sifted flour
1½ tablespoons sugar
½ teaspoon baking powder
¼ pound margarine
pinch of salt
1 egg, well beaten

Mix dry ingredients. Add margarine, then the egg, well beaten. Chill dough thoroughly in refrigerator. Roll out on wax paper. Bake at 400° to 450° for 10 to 15 minutes. Then lower to 350° until done—very flaky!

Dutch Apple Pie
Razie Abrams

2½ cups flour
1 cup sugar
½ pound sweet melted butter
1 teaspoon almond extract
4 or 5 eating apples (peeled and sliced)

Mix flour, sugar, and butter. Add almond extract and make into dough. Divide and use half for bottom of pie. Add apples and remainder of dough for top of pie. Score top with fork. Bake at 450° for 45 minutes or until top crust is golden brown.

Peach Custard Pie
Cassie Selk

1½ cups flour
1 teaspoon salt
2 tablespoons milk
1½ teaspoons sugar
½ cup oil

Mix above ingredients and press into a 9 or 10 inch pie dish.

Filling:
1 cup sugar
3 tablespoons flour added to sugar
2 eggs
3 tablespoons butter or margarine

Mix well and add 5 medium peaches sliced. Pour into pie crust. Bake in 425° oven for 40 minutes.

Pumpkin Pie
Rose Bakish

1 cup corn flake crumbs, ½ of 1 stick of margarine. Mix with 2 tablespoons of sugar. Grease pie pan. Put in crumbs—padded on bottom and sides. Bake 10 minutes at 350°.

Filling:
½ cup dried milk
2½ cups pumpkin

Add:
½ cup sugar or less
2 eggs
pinch of salt

Mix sugar and cinnamon for topping. Bake in 350° oven for 25 minutes.

Lemon Meringue Pie
Jean Reed

Mix in saucepan:
1½ cups sugar
5⅓ tablespoons cornstarch

Stir in gradually 1½ cups water. Cook over moderate heat, stirring constantly until mixture thickens and boils. Boil 1 minute.

   Slowly stir half the mixture into 3 egg yolks, slightly beaten, then beat into hot mixture in saucepan. Boil 1 minute longer, stirring constantly. Remove from heat. Continue stirring until smooth.

Blend in:
3 tablespoons butter
4 tablespoons lemon juice
1⅓ tablespoons grated lemon rind

Pour into baked pie shell. Spread meringue over filling, sealing edges onto crust. Bake 8 to 10 minutes in 400° oven until lightly browned. Cool away from drafts.

Meringue:
3 egg whites
pinch of cream of tartar
6 tablespoons sugar

Beat egg whites and cream of tartar until frothy. Continue beating, adding the sugar gradually. Beat until stiff.

Jessie Wallace's Pecan Pie
Selma Mitrani

3 eggs, slightly beaten
½ cup dark corn syrup
⅛ teaspoon salt
1 teaspoon vanilla
1 cup sugar
2 tablespoons melted margarine

Stir all together. Pour in 8 inch pie crust. Arrange whole pecans on top. Bake at 400° for 15 minutes, then 20 to 25 minutes at 350°. Test with toothpick before removing from oven.

Chocolate Pie
Cassie Selk

Blend ¾ cup milk with 2 eggs. Add 1½ cups sugar and 3 heaping tablespoons cocoa, 3 tablespoons flour, and a pinch of salt. Blend well. Add ¾ stick melted butter and 1½ teaspoon vanilla. Blend well.

   Pour into unbaked deep dish pie shell. Bake 40 minutes in 350° oven. Serve warm with ice cream. *Very attractive pie and delicious.*

Cakes and Frostings

Cheese Cake
Nina Feldser

1 pound cream cheese
⅔ cup sugar
3 tablespoons sugar
cinnamon
3 eggs
1 teaspoon vanilla
½ teaspoon almond extract
1 cup sour cream

Beat cream cheese and ⅔ cup sugar thoroughly. Add eggs, one at a time, beating well after each addition. Add almond extract. Put in a 9" pie pan. Bake at 350° oven for 25 minutes. Take out of oven and let cool for 10 minutes.

Topping:
Mix sour cream, 3 tablespoons sugar, and vanilla. Spread on top. Sprinkle with cinnamon, and put back into 350° oven
for 5 minutes.

Chocolate Devil's Food Cake
Betty Gearinger

Cream-beat well:
2 eggs
½ cup shortening
2 cups sugar

Mix well:
1 cup buttermilk
2½ cups bread flour

Mix well in hot water:
2 teaspoons baking soda
1 teaspoon salt
½ cup cocoa
1 cup hot water

Bake in 350° for 30 to 35 minutes. Test with toothpick.

After taking cake from the oven, while still hot, spread with peanut butter over the cake. Then when it cools, ice with your favorite frosting.

Poppy Seed Cake
Miriam Reisman

Mix together:
1 package Yellow cake mix
4 eggs
¾ cup oil
¾ cup poppy seeds
1 cup water
1 package instant butterscotch pudding

Beat at medium speed for 2 minutes. Bake in well-greased tube or Bunt pan at 350° for about 50 minutes or until tested done. It will be very brown and pull away from the sides of the pan.

Poor Man's Pound Cake
Mary Wright

Grease and flour 2 loaf pans
3 cups flour
3 scant teaspoons baking powder
6 unbeaten eggs
2 teaspoons almond extract or vanilla
3 cups sugar (level)
1½ cups Crisco oil
1 cup milk

Place all ingredients in a large mixing bowl. Beat 5½ minutes at medium speed. Bake 1 hour and 20 minutes or 1 hour and thirty minutes. Bake in 350° oven. (Crack on top). Take out after 10 minutes from pans.

Ricotta Cake
Gerry Romeo

Box of Marble Cake mix. Follow directions. Mix together, in separate dish, 2 pounds of Ricotta cheese, 4 eggs, ¾ cup sugar, ½ teaspoon vanilla. Beat these ingredients together until smooth.

Put cake batter in a greased 9 x 13 inch baking dish. Drop large spoonfuls on top of batter of the cheese mixture. Bake at 350° oven for 1 hour. When cake is cool, add topping.

Topping:
One whole cool whip plus 1 large box of instant chocolate pudding. This is the icing or sprinkle powdered sugar on top.

Blueberry Cake
Ida Fattman

1 can (1 pound 5-ounce) pie filling
4 eggs
3 cups flour
½ cup shortening
1 teaspoon vanilla
½ cup butter or margarine
1 teaspoon salt
1½ cups sugar
2 teaspoons baking powder

Cream sugar, shortening, and butter or margarine. Add eggs, one at a time. Add flour, salt, baking powder, and vanilla. Put ½ of dough into 9 x 13 inch pan. Add can of pie filling and rest of dough. Add topping.

Topping:
½ cup sugar
¼ cup margarine
cinnamon

Crumble and put on top. Bake cake in 350° oven for 50 to 55 minutes.

Honey and Nut Cake
Vivienne Arcus

½ cup oil
¾ cup strained honey
½ cup sugar
3 egg yolks, lightly beaten
½ cup grated walnuts
1 teaspoon vanilla
juice and rind of 1 orange

1 tablespoon cold water
2 cups sifted cake flour
1½ teaspoons baking powder
½ teaspoon soda
½ teaspoon salt
3 egg whites, beaten stiff

Mix oil, honey, sugar, yolks, nuts, orange rind, and juice, vanilla, and water. Beat well. Add flour, baking powder, soda, and salt, gradually. Beat well. Fold in whites. Bake in buttered tube pan in 375° oven for 45 minutes.

Carrot Cake
Jean Sherman

2 cups flour
2 cups sugar (or less)
2 cups carrots, grated
2 teaspoons baking soda
2 teaspoons salt
1½ cups oil
4 eggs
2 teaspoons cinnamon

Cream eggs and sugar. Add oil. Combine all dry ingredients; then add to batter. Bake in deep pan at 375° for 45 minutes.

Frosting:
¾ cup margarine
¾ package cream cheese
¾ cup confectioner's sugar

Fruit Cocktail Cake
Jennie Hasson

4 cups flour
4 teaspoons baking soda
1 cup oil
3 cups sugar (or less)
4 eggs
1 large can fruit cocktail

Drain fruit, saving juice. Add all ingredients into one bowl and mix: add juice last. Bake at 350° for 1 hour and 15 minutes. Test. If center springs back after pressing, the cake is done.

Apple Crumb Cake
Helen Collen

2½ pounds apples
  (thinly sliced on broad side of grater)
½ cup shortening
¾ cup sugar
1 egg
1 teaspoon vanilla
2 cups flour
2 teaspoons baking powder
¼ teaspoon salt
brown sugar and cinnamon

Cream shortening and sugar. Add egg, vanilla, and flour, baking powder, and salt. Spread ¾ of mixture in 7 x 11 inch oblong pan. Fill with apples. Sprinkle brown sugar and cinnamon, then add rest of crumb mixture. Bake in 350° oven for 45 minutes.

Cherry Cream Cheese Topped Cake
Ruby Lee

1 package yellow cake mix
1 envelope Dream Whip
1 (8-ounce) package cream cheese
2 cans cherry pie filling

Bake cake according to directions on package, on large cookie sheet. Allow to cool.

Topping:
Prepare 1 envelope Dream Whip according to package directions. To this add 1 package softened cream cheese, and spread over cooled cake, then spread on 2 cans cherry pie filling.

Buttermilk Cake
Rose Bakish
Madelyn's favorite

¼ pound butter or margarine
2 eggs
1½ cups sugar
pinch of salt
1 cup buttermilk
2 cups cake flour
¼ teaspoon soda
1 teaspoon vanilla

Cream butter, eggs, and sugar together. Add buttermilk and vanilla. Add flour sifted with soda and salt. Use spoon and mix well. Moist batter. Grease 9 x 13 inch baking dish and bake in 350° oven for 35 minutes or longer. (Does not need frosting.)

Nut Torte
Vivienne Arcus

Grate 2 cups pecans. Beat 4 egg yolks until thick and light. Beat in 1 cup sugar. Stir in 2 tablespoons flour, ½ teaspoon salt, ½ teaspoon baking powder, and 1 tablespoon orange juice or rum. Add nuts. Beat egg whites and fold in. Pour into two 8 inch, well-greased round pans, lined with buttered wax paper. Bake at 350° for 25 minutes. Put layers together with 1 cup whipped cream, mixed with 1½ teaspoonfuls grated orange rind.

Frosting:
Melt 6 ounces semi-sweet chocolate bits. Stir into ½ cup sour cream.

Prune Nut Cake
Helen Collen

½ cup shortening
1 cup brown sugar (tightly packed)
2 eggs
1 teaspoon baking soda
1 teaspoon cinnamon
½ cup chopped walnuts
1 cup chopped prunes
5 tablespoons prune juice
1½ cups sifted flour

Cream shortening and sugar. Add 2 eggs. Add slowly the sifted dry ingredients with the prune juice. Then add the prunes and nuts. Bake in greased oblong pan 7 x 11 inches in 350° oven, for 45 minutes.

Raisin Cake
Ruby Lee

Bring to a boil:
1 cup raisins
1½ cups water

Stir in:
1½ teaspoons baking soda

Set aside to cool for at least 1 hour.

Cream together:
2 cups sugar
1 cup oil
3 eggs

To this mixture, add alternately:
3 cups flour
liquid from raisins

Add:
1 teaspoon vanilla
½ teaspoon salt

Fold in:
1 cup raisins (boiled previously above)
1 cup nuts

Bake in a greased tube pan for 1½ hours at 350°.
Can be iced or not, as desired.

Wet Chocolate Cake
Helen Miller

½ cup shortening
2 cups sugar (or less)
2 eggs, beaten
¾ cup sour milk
2 cups flour
½ cup cocoa
pinch of salt
2 teaspoons baking soda in 1 cup hot water
1 teaspoon vanilla

Just mix ingredients in the order given. The batter is very thin. Frost with Minute Fudge Frosting.

Minute Fudge Frosting
Helen Miller

1 square (1 ounce) unsweetened chocolate, finely cut
1 cup granulated sugar
¼ cup vegetable shortening
1 teaspoon vanilla extract
⅓ cup milk
¼ teaspoon salt

Place all ingredients in saucepan (except vanilla). Bring slowly to full rolling boil, stirring constantly—boil 1 minute. Beat until lukewarm. Add vanilla and beat until thick enough to spread. Add 1 tablespoonful of cream if too thick. (Note: transfer frosting to small mixing bowl and beat with electric beater.)

Tea Time Tassies
Mary Noll

3 ounces cream cheese
1 cup flour
1 stick margarine

Filling: (mix together)
1 egg, slightly beaten
¾ cup brown sugar (firmly packed)
1 tablespoon melted margarine
1 teaspoon vanilla
dash of salt
1 cup chopped pecans

Blend together cream cheese, flour and margarine and chill before molding into cups. Mold crust into small balls with indentation and place in 1½ inch cupcake pans. Bake 350° for 20 minutes. Place 1 tablespoonful filling into each cup.
Makes 24 to 30 Tassies

Dark Chocolate Cupcakes
Jean Reed
No beating!

2 squares cooking chocolate
¼ pound butter
1 cup sugar
1 egg
milk (enough to fill 1 cup after beating egg in same—about ¾ cup)
1 cup cake flour
1½ teaspoons baking powder
½ teaspoon salt
1 teaspoon vanilla

Melt chocolate and butter in top of double boiler, then add sugar and remove from fire. Put egg in measuring cup, and beat with fork, then fill rest of cup with milk. Sift flour, baking powder, and salt and add alternately with egg mixture to chocolate mixture in pan. Add vanilla. Stir all together. Do not beat. Mixture will be almost thin enough to pour. Fill cupcake tins ½ to ⅔ full, and bake in 375° oven for 20 to 25 minutes. Frost with chocolate frosting.

Cream Cheese Cupcakes
Mary Noll

3 (8-ounce) packages Kraft cream cheese
5 eggs
1 cup sugar
¼ teaspoon vanilla

Cream eggs and cheese. Beat in sugar and vanilla. Pour in paper lined cupcake pans. Bake in 300° oven for 40 minutes. Cool 5 minutes. Put on topping and bake 5 more minutes.

Topping: (mix together)
1 cup sour cream
¼ cup sugar
¼ teaspoon vanilla
add a dot of jelly on top

Fluffy White Frosting
Cassie Selk

1 cup sugar
⅛ teaspoon salt
1 teaspoon light corn syrup
½ teaspoon vanilla
¼ teaspoon cream of tartar
⅓ cup water
1 egg white

Stir sugar, cream of tartar, salt, water, and corn syrup together. Bring to a boil and boil for about 1 minute.

Break egg white into small mixing bowl and whip. Pour hot syrup over egg white and beat until spreading consistency. Add one-half teaspoon vanilla.

Pecan Tarts
Vivienne Arcus

Butter 18 muffin tins. Preheat oven later to 350°. Let stand at room temperature for one hour: 1 stick of butter or margarine and 1 small (3-ounce) cream cheese. Blend with fork or wooden spoon. Add pinch of salt. Add flour in small amounts and keep using fork or wooden spoon and also work with fingers until dough is thick enough to divide.

Divide dough into 18 equal parts. Put each ball in bottom of muffin tins. Make paper thin and spread over sides and bottom (no holes in bottom). Sprinkle 1 tablespoonful of chopped pecans over dough.

Filling:
Place 3 eggs in bowl and beat with fork. Add 2¼ cups of lightly packed light brown sugar, 3 or 4 tablespoonfuls of melted butter or margarine and 1 teaspoon vanilla. Mix and pour over nuts. Put one or two pecans over top of each tart. Bake 15 minutes in 350° oven, lower temperature to 250° and bake 10 or 15 minutes more.
Very attractive company dessert and also delicious.

Coconut Frosting
Jennie Hasson

½ **stick margarine**
1 **small can of condensed milk**
¾ **cup sugar**
1 **teaspoon vanilla**
1 **large box Baker's sweetened coconut**

Melt margarine, add sugar and milk. Boil for 1 minute. Stir in vanilla and coconut. Mix well and spread over cold cake.

Butter Icing
Cassie Selk

½ **stick butter (or ¼ butter and ¼ margarine)**
⅛ **teaspoon salt**
2 **cups powdered sugar**
¼ **cup milk**
1 **teaspoon vanilla**

Beat ingredients until soft, then add 2 cups powdered sugar. Boil one-fourth cup milk and add to sugar mixture. Add 1 teaspoon vanilla and mix well. Spread icing over cooled cake or other baked goods.

Cream Cheese Icing for Zucchini, Banana, and Nut Breads
Iris Levy

1 **8-ounce package cream cheese**
1 **cup confectioner's sugar**
2 **tablespoons butter or margarine**
1 **teaspoon vanilla**

Mix all ingredients and add a little lemon juice. (Good icing for different types of breads.)

Creamy Chocolate Frosting
Jean Reed

½ cup butter or margarine
1 egg
½ cup cocoa
¼ teaspoon salt
4 cups confectioner's sugar
1 teaspoon vanilla
⅓ cup milk

Blend butter, egg, cocoa, and salt. Add sugar alternately with milk and vanilla, mixing until smooth and creamy. Makes enough to frost layer cake.

Chocolate Frosting
Vivienne Arcus

Combine 1 cup Nestle's Quick chocolate, ½ cup softened butter or margarine, ¼ cup boiling water, and ½ teaspoon vanilla. Gradually blend in 2¼ cups confectioner's sugar. Beat until thick.

Cookies

Easy Macaroons
Mary Wright

2 8-ounce packages of shredded coconut
   (or large 15-ounce package)
1 15-ounce can Eagle Brand milk
2 teaspoons vanilla

Mix all together and drop spoonfuls on Teflon pan. Bake in 350° oven for 10 to 12 minutes. Cool slightly.
Makes 4 dozen

Buttermilk Cookies
Joanna Buckingham

1 heaping cup of sugar
½ cup shortening (heaping and rounded)

Add:
1 unbeaten egg
1 tablespoon vanilla
   (orange or lemon flavoring)
½ cup buttermilk (running over generously)
1 level cup flour
1 teaspoon salt (scant)
1 teaspoon baking powder
½ teaspoon baking soda

Then add:
1½ cups flour

Drop by tablespoonful on baking sheet and pat with glass and sprinkle with sugar. Bake in 425° oven for 8 to 10 minutes.

Sesame Cookies
Gerry Romeo

4 cups and 1 tablespoon flour
½ teaspoon salt
2 cups sugar (or less)
2 eggs
2 teaspoons baking powder
8 ounces shortening, butter, or margarine
½ cup milk

Mix shortening and sugar. Stir in eggs and milk, a little bit at a time. Add flour sifted with baking powder and salt. Place in refrigerator for ½ to 1 hour.

Grease cookie sheet and shape dough and roll in hands making little logs. Roll in sesame seeds. Bake in 350° oven from 10 to 15 minutes.

Old-Fashioned Rocks
Liz Sturgeon

Mix:
1½ cups brown sugar
1 cup shortening
2 beaten eggs
¼ cup raisin liquid
1 teaspoon cinnamon
½ teaspoon cloves
1 teaspoon soda
3 cups flour
½ teaspoon salt
1 cup raisins
½ cup nuts (optional)

Put raisins in 1 cup water and boil until soft. Save ¼ cup liquid. Mix. Nuts are optional. Bake for 350° for about 10 minutes.

Chocolate Chip Bars
Ida Fattman

1¼ cups or 1½ cups graham cracker crumbs
1 stick sweet butter or margarine
1 cup chopped nuts
1 cup chocolate chips (or butterscotch)
1¼ cups Angel food coconut
1 can condensed milk

Place stick of butter in pan and melt in oven. Sprinkle graham cracker crumbs over melted butter. Take coconut and sprinkle over batter. Take chocolate chips and do the same—also nuts. Dribble 1 can of condensed milk over all to cover.

For thinner cookies, use 9 x 13 pan. For thicker cookies, use 7 x 11 inch pan. Bake in 350° for 30 to 35 minutes. Cut into squares after cooling.

Fudgies (No Bake Cookies)
Lois Sturgeon

Bring to a boil:
2 cups sugar
3 tablespoons cocoa
½ cup milk
¼ pound butter or margarine

Add:
½ cup peanut butter
1 teaspoon vanilla

Stir until melted. Then add:
3 cups rolled oats (uncooked)

Drop by spoonful on cookie sheet or spread in greased sheet pan and cut in squares.

Cottage Cheese Cookies
Vivienne Arcus

Mix and refrigerate overnight:
½ **pound butter**
2 **cups flour**
pinch of salt
½ **pound creamed cottage cheese**

Next day: Divide dough into 4 portions. Remove one portion at a time from refrigerator. Keep rest chilled until needed. When cookies are shaped, place cookie sheets in refrigerator about ½ hour before baking.

Roll paper thin on floured board. Cut into 1½ inch squares. Fill center of each with a dab of strawberry or pineapple preserves. Pinch two opposite corners together. Then pinch the other 2 corners together to form little "pillows." Bake in 400° oven for about 10 minutes; then lower to 350° until flaky and puffy. When cool, sift confectioner's sugar on top.

Applesauce Cookies
Lois Sturgeon

Cream together:
¾ **cup shortening**
1 **cup brown sugar**

Add:
1 **egg and beat**
½ **cup applesauce**

Sift together:
2¼ **cups sifted flour**
½ **teaspoon each: soda, salt**
¾ **teaspoon cinnamon**
¼ **teaspoon cloves**

Add to above:
1 **cup raisins** (Cook 1 cup raisins in boiling water till soft. Drain and cool.)

Drop batter by teaspoon onto greased cookie sheet. Bake in 350° oven for 10 to 12 minutes.

Bon Bon Cookies
Naomi Heskel

½ **cup Crisco**
1 **cup sugar**
1 **teaspoon vanilla**
½ **cup margarine (parvu)**
1 **egg yolk**
2 **cups flour**

Cream margarine, shortening, and sugar together. Add egg yolk, vanilla, and flour. Mix well until light. Roll into balls. Do not flatten. Place on ungreased cookie sheet in 350° oven for 20 to 30 minutes until bottom is light brown.
Makes 6 dozen
Delicious!

Fruit Bars
Lois Sturgeon

Cream:
½ **cup shortening**
1 **cup sugar**

Mix:
1 **egg**
¼ **cup orange or pineapple juice**

Add to first 2 ingredients. Mix thoroughly.
(sift together) Then add:
2½ cups flour
½ teaspoon salt
1 teaspoon soda
½ teaspoon cinnamon
½ teaspoon nutmeg

Add:
1 cup candied fruit
1 cup chopped dates (or raisins)
½ cup chopped nuts

Divide dough in half. Roll on floured board. Make oblong shapes, approx. 7 x 12 inches. Cut into strips (2 inches wide) and lay on greased cookie sheet. Do the same with rest of dough. Bake at 375° (or 350°) for 12 minutes.

When cool, frost with vanilla-butter-powdered sugar icing. Cut into bars.

Apricot Squares
Vivienne Arcus
A delicious shortbread-type crumbly cookie.

Cook 1 pound box dried apricots until mushy. Add sugar and lemon juice to individual taste; cool.

Mix by hand:
¼ pound butter
2½ cups flour
4 heaping tablespoons sugar
4 yolks
1½ teaspoons baking powder
1 teaspoon vanilla

Cream butter and sugar by hand. Add 1 yolk at a time. Add flour, sugar, baking powder, and vanilla. Take off a little more than ⅓ of dough and reserve. Pat remainder of dough with floured hand on

bottom of 9 x 13 inch pan. Pour apricot mixture over dough. Roll remainder of dough into pencil-thin strips and criss-cross over filling, making about 2 inch squares.

Bake at 350° oven until lightly browned—about 45 minutes to 1 hour. Cut through strips while hot to form squares.

Mandelbrot
Esther Ann Zabitz

Preheat over to 350°. Cookie sheets can either be 10 x 15 (2 loaves) or 15 x 14 (3 loaves)
Use cookie sheets or jelly roll pans. Combine in order. Set mixer at medium speed.

3 eggs
1½ teaspoons baking powder
1½ teaspoons almond extract
¼ teaspoon salt
1 cup sugar
¼ cup finely ground walnuts
1 cup Hollywood Safflower oil
3 cups flour

The dough will be very, very stiff depending on the size of the eggs. Form the dough into loaves leaving a 2 inch space between loaves. Bake for 15 minutes. Remove from oven and immediately while it is still hot start slicing using a sharp knife. Arrange the slices so that the unbaked side is face up. You may need to use a second cookie sheet. Return the cookie sheets to the oven for another 15 mintues. Slices should be nicely browned.

The number of slices you get from a loaf varies. If you are using the 2 loaf pan you should get about 15 slices. If you are using the 3 loaf size you should get about 10 slices to a loaf. However a lot depends upon the size of the eggs and the quality of the flour.

Soft Molasses Cookies
Dorothy Wilson

2¼ cups flour
1 teaspoon ginger
1 teaspoon cinnamon
¼ teaspoon salt
2 teaspoons baking soda
2 tablespoons hot water
½ cup soft shortening
½ cup granulated sugar
½ cup molasses
1 egg
6 tablespoons cold water
½ cup seedless raisins

Heat oven to 350°. Sift together first 4 ingredients. Dissolve soda in hot water. Mix shortening and next 3 ingredients until creamy, mix in flour mixture alternately with cold water; then mix in soda and raisins, if desired, or put raisins on top of cookies, after dropping by rounded tablespoonfuls 2" apart onto greased cookie sheet. Sprinkle with sugar. Bake 13 to 14 minutes.
Great molasses taste.

Anise Drops
Connie Frohman

1½ cups sifted flour
¼ teaspoon baking powder
2 eggs (add water to make ½ cup liquid)
1 cup sugar
¼ teaspoon anise flavoring

Generously grease cookie sheets. Sift together flour and baking powder. Put eggs into large bowl with sugar and anise. Beat until very thick and piled softly. Fold in dry ingredients, sifting in ¼ at a time. Drop by teaspoonfuls onto cookie sheets

about 2" apart. Set cookie sheets aside in a cool place. (Do not refrigerate.) Leave dough out for 8 to 10 hours overnight. Do not cover and do not disturb. Bake at 350° for 5 to 6 minutes. Cool on racks.
Makes about 4 dozen

Hamentashen
Ruth Schwimmer

Dough:
⅓ cup oil
¼ cup orange juice
1 cup sugar
3 eggs
2 teaspoons baking powder
¼ teaspoon salt
3 (plus) cups flour (until you can roll dough ½ inch thick)

Place filling on dough circle. (Use glass to cut.) Pinch into triangular shape. Bake at 375° for 20 minutes.

Filling:
prune butter (or cook prunes in a little water until thick—remove pits)
nuts
lemon juice

Strudel
Vivienne Arcus

½ pound butter
1 egg yolk
2 cups flour
1 cup sour cream

Mix together and refrigerate overnight. Next day: Divide dough into 4 portions. Take one piece at a time from refrigerator and roll paper thin. Spread each piece generously with sugar, cinnamon, nuts, raisins, and dot generously with butter (thinly sliced apples optional). Roll jelly roll fashion. Pinch ends together and place on cookie sheet. Brush top with either egg white or whole beaten egg.

Bake in preheated 400° oven for 10 to 15 minutes. Then lower to 350° and bake approximately another 45 minutes until brown. After shaping, strudel rolls will be flakier if placed in refrigerator about ½ hour before baking.

Crescent Nut Cookies
Rose Bakish
No eggs or milk.

Mix together:
2 sticks margarine (parvu)
2 cups flour
½ cup sugar
1 teaspoon vanilla
½ cup finely chopped nuts

Let rest in the refrigerator for 1 hour. Take some dough, about the size of a marble, and push thumb in the side and make it form into a crescent. Should look like a half moon.

Bake on a greased pan in a 350° oven for 16 to 18 minutes. Roll in powdered sugar, optional.
Melts in one's mouth.

Lemon Lush
Reina Bakish

½ cup chopped pecans
¼ pound butter, melted
1 cup flour

Mix together. Press into bottom of greased 9 x 13 pan. Bake at 350° for 15 minutes. Let cool. Mix:

1 (8-ounce) package cream cheese
1 cup Cool Whip
1 cup confectioner's sugar

Beat well and spread on cooled crust. Mix:

2 packages lemon instant pudding
3 cups milk

Spread on cake. Optional: Spread cool whip on top as icing.
Truly luscious.

Apple Nut Cake
Reina Bakish

Beat together:
2 cups sugar (or less)
1½ cups oil

Add:
3 eggs (beat until creamy)
1 teaspoon vanilla

Add:
3 cups sifted flour
1 teaspoon salt
1 teaspoon baking soda
1 teaspoon cinnamon
Batter becomes very thick.

Fold in:
1 to 1½ cups chopped walnuts
3 cups raw, peeled, diced apples
   (approx. 4 apples)

Grease and flour bundt pan or tube pan. Sprinkle empty pan with 2 tablespoons cinnamon and sugar mixture. Add batter. Bake at 350° for approximately 1 hour (depending on moistness desired). Turn off oven. Let cake in about 15 minutes more. Cool cake. Turn upside down when cooled.

See what 40 years can do. Same sister and brother. (1914, 1954).

INDEX

Recipe Index

Almond-Rice Stuffing or Casserole, 112

Anise Drops, 136

Apple Cake, 18

Apple Cake, Jewish, 61

Apple Coffee Cake, 61

Apple Crisp, 122

Apple Crumb Cake, 127

Apple Crunch, Crispy, 78

Apple Nut Cake, 138

Apple Pie Crust, 25

Apple Pie Filling, 25

Apple Pie, Crazy Crust, 122

Apple Strudel, 26

Applesauce, 78

Applesauce Cookies, 134

Applesauce, Home-Made, 55

Apricot Chicken Breasts, 104

Apricot Squares, 135

Bagels, Passover, 84

Baked Beans, 23

Baked Beans, Quick, 23

Baked Cheese and Egg Dish, 115

Baked Chicken, Lazy, 39

Baked Chicken with Corn Flake Crumbs, 34

Baked Cranberry Sauce, 78

Baked Fish (Flounder, Sole, Haddock), 44

Baked Fish Fillets Parmesan, 109

Baked Fryers, 29

Baked Onions, 100

Baked Squash, 101

Baked Veal, Russian Style, 44

Banana Bread, 56

Banana Muffins, 120

Banana-Nut Cake, 68

Barbecued Chicken, 103

Barbecued Ground Beef, 107

Barbecued Lamb Breast (or Beef Short-Ribs), 43

Bean Casserole, Fresh, 110

Beef and Eggplant (Greek Musaca), 42

Beef and Rice Bake, 106

Beef Soup with Navy Beans, 15

Beeft Borscht, 11

Beeft Borscht (Dairy), 29

Beeft Borscht, Perfect (Meatless), 28

Black Bean Soup, 98

Blintz Torte, 66

Blintzes, 14

Blintzes, 114

Blueberry Cake, 126

Blueberry Cheese Pie, 60

Blueberry Cobbler, Fresh, 58

Blueberry-Cheesecake Dessert, 60

Boiled Bulgur, 111

Boiled Tongue, 105

Bon Bon Cookies, 134

Bonnie Butter Cake, 68

Braised Zucchini, 101

Bread Pudding, 120

Bread Rolls, 6

Bread Stuffing, 24

Brisket, 37

Broccoli and Zucchini Soup, 47

Broccoli Casserole, 51

Broiled Fish (Greek Style), 109

Broiled Salmon Steak or Fillet, 45

Broiled Trout or Whiting Fish, 45

Brown Sugar Cookies, 24

Brown Sugar Cookies #2, 25

Brown Sugar Meringue Frosting, 64

Brown Sugar Pecan Rounds, 74

Brownies, 69

Brownies, Light, 70

Buckwheat Grits, 12

Butter Frosting, 70

Butter Icing, 131

Buttermilk Cake, 128

Buttermilk Cookies, 132

Butternut Squash, 51

Butterscotch Icing, 68

Cabbage Borscht, 11

Cabbage Borscht, 99

Cabbage Salad, 49

Cabbage Soup, 11

California Chicken Divan, 102

Canned Beef Borscht, 12

Caramel Frosting, Easy, 64

Carrot Cake, 79

Carrot Cake, 127

Carrot Cookies, 25

Celery Knobs, 89

Chafing Dish Meatballs, 42

Challah Sabbath Twists, 117

Challah, Never-Fail, 119

Charoses—Passover, 81

Cheese Bagalach, 7

Cheese Blintzes, 27

Cheese Cake, 60

Cheese Cake, 125

Cheese Pit, Eleanor Deutsh's, 114

Cheese Rolls, Famous, 8

Cheese Straws, 94

Cheesies, 91

Cherry Cream Cheese Topped Cake, 128

Cherry Cream Pie, 21

Chicken Breasts in Marsala Wine, 103

Chicken Diable, 39

Chicken Fat, 11

Chicken or Beef Chow Mein, 102

Chicken Soup, 12

Chicken, Everybody's Favorite, 35

Chicken, Four-Way (Israeli Style), 35

Chili, 77

Chili, 105

Chili Con Carne, 40

Chinese Chicken Breast with Vegetables, 36

Chinese Fried Rice, 113

Chinese Sauce for Vegetables, 37

Chinese Steak, 104

Chocolate Cake, 20

Chocolate Cake, 63

Chocolate Cake #2, Wacky, 64

Chocolate Cake, Wacky, 63

Chocolate Chip Bars, 27

Chocolate Chip Bars, 133

Chocolate Chip Coffee Cake, 119

Chocolate Chip Cookies, 19

Chocolate Chip Cookies, 76

Chocolate Devil's Food Cake, 125

Chocolate Frosting, 132

Chocolate Frosting, 21

Chocolate Fudge, Favorite, 16

Chocolate Pie, 124

Chocolate Vanilla Frosting, 62

Chop Suey, Quick and Easy, 108

Chopped Liver, 11

Chopped Liver Appetizer, 94

Chopped Meat Sauce for Spaghetti, 108

Chopped Onions in Mazola Oil, 13

Chuck Roast, 36

Chuck Stew, 24

Cinnamon Frosted Zucchini Bars, 70

Cinnamon Frosting, 70

Cinnamon Twists, 58

Cocoa Brownies, 69

Cocoa Drop Cookies, 73

Cocoa Icing, 62

Cocoa Icing, Simple, 63

Coconut Frosting , 131

Cole Slaw, 98

Congo Squares, 71

Corn and Broccoli Casserole, 110

Corn and Lima Bean Chowder (Dairy), 48

Corn Meal Cookies, 74

Cottage Cheese and Noodle Dish, Easy, 47

Cottage Cheese Cookies, 134

Cottage Cheese Dumplings, 10

Cottage Cheese Jell-O Mold, 97

Cottage Cheese Pudding, 10

Crane Pumpkin Bread, 116

Cream Cheese Cupcakes, 130

Cream Cheese Icing for Zucchini, Banana, and Nut Breads, 131

Creamed Onions, 100

Creamed Sole or Haddock, 44

Creamy Chocolate Frosting, 132

Creamy Pumpkin Soup, 17

Creamy Vanilla Frosting, 62

Crescent Nut Cookies, 137

Crispy Chicken, Easy, 35

Crunchy Pea Salad, 98

Cucumber Salad, 52

Curried Chicken, 103

Dairy Kugel, 111

Danish Meat Balls, 107

Dark Chocolate Cupcakes, 130

Date Bars, 27

Date Bars, 71

Dinette Cake, 66

Dutch Apple Pie, 123

Egg Drops, 82

Egg Kichlech, 118

Egg Yolk Icing, 66

Eggplant Appetizer, 10

Eggplant Appetizer, 90

Eggplant Parmigiana, 32

Eggplant Pie, 88

Eggplant Pudding, 89

Farfel Pancakes, 84

Fikonicas (Greek-Style Cholent), 37

Fillet of Sole, 24

Fish, Fabulous, 26

Flanken (Short Ribs), 104

Flooden (Lena Lerner's favorite Purim dessert), 4

Fluffy White Frosting, 130

Fluffy White Frosting, 67

Frankfurter and Bean Casserole, 108

Frankfurters and Sauerkraut, 108

Freezer Raspberry and Strawberry Jams, 55

French Apple Pie, 59

French Dressing, 28

French Dressing, 50

French Silk Frosting, 68

Fresh Fruit Pie, Deep Dish, 59

Fried Fish (Flounder, Haddock, Sole or Trout), 45

Fried Liver in Sweet and Sour Sauce, 105

Frozen Cinnamon Apples, 96

Frozen Strawberries, Home-Made, 55

Frozen Vegetables with Gefilte Fish, 14

Fruit Bars, 134

Fruit Cocktail Cake, 127

Fruit or Lemon Squares, 121

Fruit Salad, 97

Fudge Icing, 62

Fudgies (No Bake Cookies), 133

Funnel Cakes, Amish, 115

Garlic Crackers (dairy), 96
Garlic Pasta Salad, 30
Gefilte Fish, 14
Gingersnap Cookies, 74
Givéch (Cooked vegetable salad), 22
Golden Layer Cake, Best All Around Cake, 61
Grape Jam, 55
Grape Juice Fresh From Garden, Home-Made, 54
Grape Vine Rolls, 90
Greek Lamb with String Beans, 43
Green Tomatoes with Ground Beef, 92
Ground Beef Macaroni Casserole, 42
Ground Beef with Macaroni, 15
Hamburger Patties (Lena Lerner's Specialty), 9
Hamentaschen, 77
Hamentaschen & Flacht Dough, 20
Hamentashen, 136
Hanukkah Cookies, 72
Hawaiian Pineapple Cake, 67
Herb Chicken, Garden Fresh, 34
Honey and Nut Cake, 126
Honey Cake, 5
Honey Cake, 31
Honey Cake #2, 7
Honey Poppy Seed Dressing, 31
Ice Cream Pie, 17
Israeli Chicken, 39
Italian Spaghetti and Meat Balls, 38
Jelly Roll, 6
Jelly Roll (Sponge), 6
Kamesh Bread, 5
Kamesh Brot, 19
Kasha, 38
Kasha with Shell Macaroni, 15
Kicklach (Puffy Egg Cookies), 5
Kneidlach (Matzo Balls), 9
Knishes, 106

Kohlrabi, 91
Kreplach, 10
Lamb Pilaf, 42
Lasagna, 107
Leek Patties, 90
Leeks, 89
Lemon Curd Squares, 120
Lemon Lush, 137
Lemon Meringue Pie, 124
Lemon Sponge Pie, 122
Lemon Swirl Frosting, 79
Lentil Soup, Easy, 91
Lettuce Soup (with Peas), 99
Lime-Sour Cream Mold, 97
Liver Patties, 11
London Broil, 36
London Broil in a Wok, 37
M and M Cookies, 77
Macaroni and Cheese Dish, Easy, 14
Macaroni Salad, Easy, 50
Macaroons, Easy, 132
Mamaliga—Cheese and Butter, 9
Mandel Bread, 20
Mandelbrot, 135
Marble Cake, 62
Marble Coffee Cake, 18
Marie's Chocolate Icing, 69
Marinated Carrots, 101
Marinated Mixed Vegetables, 100
Marinated Potato Salad, 98
Marinated Raw Mushrooms, 95
Marshmallow Candy, 5
Matzo Balls, Best, 82
Matzo Brie (Fried Matzo), 81
Matzo Charlotte—Passover, 84
Matzo Meal Blintzes, 85
Matzo Meal Coating for Roast Chicken, 83
Matzo Meal Omelet, 86
Matzo Meal Pancakes, 84

Matzo Pudding, Passover, 85
Meat Loaf, 31
Meat Loaf, Famous, 23
Meat-Spinach Soufflé, 88
Meringues or Kisses, 87
Microwave Coq Au Vin (Chicken), 102
Minute Fudge Frosting, 129
Mohn (Poppy Seed) Shortbread, 118
Mondel Bread, 20
Monterey Pasta, Right-Away, 48
Moussaka (Eastern Casserole), 88
Mushroom Stuffing, Passover, 83
New York Frankfurters, 38
Non-Fat Egg Rolls, 116
Noodle Kugel, Mrs. Kantor's Fabulous, 112
Noodle Pudding, 8
Noodle Pudding, 18
Noodle Pudding, 26
Noodle Pudding, Adath, 30
Noodle Rice Pilaf, 113
Noodle-Vegetable Cheese Casserole, 77
Nut Torte, 128
Oatmeal Cookies, Famous, 75
Oatmeal Coolies, Peek-A-Boo, 73
Oatmeal Crisps, 72
Oatmeal Pancakes, 11
Oatmeal Spice Cake, 65
Oil Free Eggplant, 51
Oil Pastry, 58
Old-Fashioned Rocks, 133
Old-Time Cinnamon Jumbles, 75
One-Eyed Pete, 115
Orange Sherbet Dessert, 120
Orange-Lemon Halibut Steaks, 109
Oven Baked Chicken, 102
Paella (Mexican dish), 54
Paper Thin Pancakes, 115
Paprika Schnitzel, 44
Parsley Pareve Potatoes, 84

Pastry for Pie, Delicious, 123
Pea Soup with Beef, 16
Peach Custard Pie, 123
Peach Sauce, Fresh, 121
Peanut Butter Balls, 76
Peanut Butter Broiled Topping, 65
Peanut Butter Candy, 122
Peanut Butter Cookies, 74
Peanut Butter Icing, 62
Pear Cake, 30
Pecan Balls, 28
Pecan Pie, 33
Pecan Pie, Jessie Wallace's, 124
Pecan Tarts, 131
Penuche Icing, 63
Pesach Meeana (Liver Dish), 9
Pesach Popovers, 8
Pickled Beefts, 100
Pickled Cabbage, 101
Pickles (Green Plum Tomatoes or Green
    Pickles), 21
Pie Crust, Perfect, 122
Pineapple Dessert, 121
Pineapple Zucchini Bread, 57
Pinwheel Cookies, 72
Popovers, Best Passover, 82
Poppy Seed Cake, 125
Poppy Seed Cookies, Famous, 22
Potato Latkes, 54
Potato Latkes, Uncle Miltie's, 110
Potato Liver Knishes, 106
Potato Noodles (Shlishkas), 111
Potato Soup, 99
Pound Cake, Poor Man's, 126
Procas (Stuffed Cabbage Leaves), 13
Processor Orange Bread, 117
Prune Nut Cake, 128
Puffs, Small "Duchess", 96
Pumpkin Bread, 118
Pumpkin Pie, 124

Pumpkin Pie, Fresh, 58
Punch #2, Champagne, 93
Punch, Champagne, 93
Punch, Cold Duck, 94
Punch, Green Colored, 56
Punch, Open-House, 55
Punch, Southern Comfort, 94
Punch, Thoenen's, 56
Quiche Lorraine, 114
Raisin Cake, 129
Raspberry Jam, Home-Made, 55
Rhubarb Crunch Coffee Cake, 118
Rib Roast of Beef, 104
Rice Cakes, 112
Rice Pudding, 8
Rice Pudding, 113
Richmond Chocolate Frosting, 66
Ricotta Cake, 126
Roast Beef, 13
Roast Brisket or Chuck Roast, 20
Roast Chicken, 22
Roast Chicken, 83
Roast Chicken with Rice, 13
Roast Turkey or Chicken, 12
Roasted Eggs, 90
Rocky Road Bars, 32
Rolled Roast, 12
Rolled Roast, 36
Russian Fruit Salad, 95
Russian Meat Balls, 39
Salad, Sunshine, 49
Salmon Loaf, 16
Salmon Loaf, 28
Scalloped Apples, 96
Scalloped Tomatoes, 51
Sea Breeze Drink, 94
Sesame Cookies, 133
Sliced Cucumber Pickles, 52
Sliced Cucumber Pickles, 95
Smoked Salmon, Hot, 80

Snowflakes, 4
Soft Molasses Cookies, 136
"Souper" Chicken, 40
Sour Cream Nut Cake, 92
Spanish Rice (Mexican dish), 54
Spice Cake, Quick-Method, 64
Spicy Rhubarb Cake, 79
Spicy Zucchini Cake, 79
Spinach and Rice, 113
Spinach Kugel, 19
Spinach Pudding, 89
Spinach-Meat Patties, 90
Sponge Cake, Best Passover, 86
Squash Fritters, 53
Stewed String Beans, 50
Stir-Fry Chicken in Wine Sauce, 103
Strawberries Romanoff, 121
Strawberry Jam, 55
Strudel, 136
Stuffed Breast of Veal, 43
Stuffed Cabbage, 106
Stuffed Cabbage Leaves and Cabbage
    Soup, 40
Stuffed Mushrooms, 52
Stuffed Pasta Shells, 78
Stuffed Zucchini with Ground Beef, 41
Stuffing for Veal Breast, 43
Summer Squash, Sandwich Pickles, 22
Sweet and Sour Sauce, 41
Sweet and Sour Stuffed Peppers, 40
Sweet Potatoes Candied with Brown
    Sugar, 49
Sweet Rolls, 6
Taglach Dumplings, 24
Tea Kettle Tea, 13
Tea Time Tassies, 130
Toasted Farfel for Soup, 82
Tomato Sauce for Gefilte Fish, 14
Tomato Sauce, Summer, 46
Tomato Soup, 100

Tsimmes, 111
Trout in Envelopes for Two, 45
Tuna Bread, Hot, 45
Tuna Hot Dish, 29
Tuna, Noodle, and Mushroom Soup Casserole, 46
Tutti Frutti Squares, 71
Veal Chops, 26
Veal Steak in Tomato Sauce, 44
Vegetable Casserole, 110
Vegetable Dip, Easy, 95
Vegetable Soup, 99
Vegetable Soup, 99
Vegetables, Beautiful Winter, 101
Vichyssoise Soup, 100
Walnut Snack, 52
Washboard Cookies, 76
Wet Chocolate Cake, 129
Whiskey Sour, 94
White Cake with Grated Chocolate (Ski Cake), 65
White Icing, 64
Yum Yums, 97
Zucchini Bread, 56
Zucchini Casserole, 29
Zucchini Muffins, 57
Zucchini Squash and Cheese Casserole, 89
Zucchini Vegetable Soup, 48
Zucchini Walnut Bread, 56
Zucchini with Pasta, 53
Zucchini-Bean Stir-Fry, 53
Zucchini-Pineapple Bread, 32
Zucchini-Spaghetti Soup, 54

Category Index

BEEF

Barbecued Ground Beef, 107
Beef and Rice Bake, 106
Boiled Tongue, 105
Brisket, 37
Chafing Dish Meatballs, 42
Chicken, Everybody's Favorite, 35
Chili, 77
Chili, 105
Chili Con Carne, 40
Chinese Steak, 104
Chuck Roast, 36
Chuck Stew, 24
Danish Meat Balls, 107
Fikonicas (Greek-Style Cholent), 37
Flanken (Short Ribs), 104
Frankfurters and Sauerkraut, 108
Green Tomatoes with Ground Beef, 92
Ground Beef with Macaroni, 15
Hamburger Patties (Lena Lerner's Specialty), 9
Italian Spaghetti and Meat Balls, 38
London Broil, 36
London Broil in a Wok, 37
Meat Loaf, 31
Meat Loaf, Famous, 23
Meat-Spinach Soufflé, 88
New York Frankfurters, 38
Rib Roast of Beef, 104
Roast Beef, 13
Roast Brisket or Chuck Roast, 20
Rolled Roast, 12
Rolled Roast, 36
Russian Meat Balls, 39
Spinach-Meat Patties, 90
Stuffed Zucchini with Ground Beef, 41

BREADS, MUFFINS, MATZO

Bagels, Passover, 84
Banana Bread, 56
Banana Muffins, 120
Bread Rolls, 6
Challah Sabbath Twists, 117
Challah, Never-Fail, 119
Crane Pumpkin Bread, 116
Dairy Kugel, 111
Garlic Crackers (dairy), 96
Kamesh Bread, 5
Kamesh Brot, 19
Kneidlach (Matzo Balls), 9
Kreplach, 10
Mandel Bread, 19
Mandlebrot, 135
Matzo Balls, Best, 82
Matzo Brie (Fried Matzo), 81
Matzo Charlotte—Passover, 84
Mohn (Poppy Seed) Shortbread, 118
Mondel Bread, 20
Noodle Kugel, Mrs. Kantor's Fabulous, 112
Pesach Popovers, 8
Pineapple Zucchini Bread, 57
Popovers, Best Passover, 82
Processor Orange Bread, 117
Pumpkin Bread, 118
Spinach Kugel, 19
Taglach Dumplings, 24
Tuna Bread, Hot, 45
Zucchini Bread, 56
Zucchini Muffins, 57
Zucchini Walnut Bread, 56
Zucchini-Pineapple Bread, 32

CAKES

Apple Cake, 18
Apple Cake, Jewish, 61
Apple Coffee Cake, 61
Apple Crumb Cake, 127
Apple Nut Cake, 138
Banana-Nut Cake, 68
Blueberry Cake, 126
Blueberry-Cheesecake Dessert, 60
Bonnie Butter Cake, 68

Buttermilk Cake, 128
Carrot Cake, 79
Carrot Cake, 127
Cheese Cake, 60
Cheese Cake, 125
Cherry Cream Cheese Topped Cake, 128
Chocolate Cake, 20
Chocolate Cake, 63
Chocolate Cake #2, Wacky, 64
Chocolate Cake, Wacky, 63
Chocolate Chip Coffee Cake, 119
Chocolate Devil's Food Cake, 125
Cream Cheese Cupcakes, 130
Dark Chocolate Cupcakes, 130
Dinette Cake, 66
Fruit Cocktail Cake, 127
Funnel Cakes, Amish, 115
Golden Layer Cake, Best All Around
    Cake, 61
Hawaiian Pineapple Cake, 67
Honey and Nut Cake, 126
Honey Cake, 5
Honey Cake, 31
Honey Cake #2, 7
Marble Cake, 62
Marble Coffee Cake, 18
Nut Torte, 128
Oatmeal Pancakes, 11
Oatmeal Spice Cake, 65
Pear Cake, 30
Poppy Seed Cake, 125
Pound Cake, Poor Man's, 126
Prune Nut Cake, 128
Raisin Cake, 129
Rhubarb Crunch Coffee Cake, 118
Rice Cakes, 112
Ricotta Cake, 126
Sour Cream Nut Cake, 92
Spice Cake, Quick-Method, 64
Spicy Rhubarb Cake, 79

Spicy Zucchini Cake, 79
Sponge Cake, Best Passover, 86
Wet Chocolate Cake, 129
White Cake with Grated Chocolate
    (Ski Cake), 65

CASSEROLES
Bean Casserole, Fresh, 110
Broccoli Casserole, 51
Corn and Broccoli Casserole, 110
Frankfurter and Bean Casserole, 108
Ground Beef Macaroni Casserole, 42
Moussaka (Eastern Casserole), 88
Noodle-Vegetable Cheese Casserole, 77
Tsimmes, 111
Tuna, Noodle, and Mushroom Soup
    Casserole, 46
Vegetable Casserole, 110
Zucchini Casserole, 29
Zucchini Squash and Cheese Casserole, 89

CHEESE DISHES
Baked Cheese and Egg Dish, 115
Blintz Torte, 66
Blintzes, 14
Blintzes, 114
Cheese Bagalach, 7
Cheese Blintzes, 27

Cheese Pit, Eleanor Deutsh's, 114
Cheese Rolls, Famous, 8
Cheese Straws, 94
Cheesies, 91
Cottage Cheese and Noodle Dish,
    Easy, 47
Cottage Cheese Dumplings, 10
Lasagna, 107
Macaroni and Cheese Dish, Easy, 14
Mamaliga—Cheese and Butter, 9
Matzo Meal Blintzes, 85
Quiche Lorraine, 114

CHICKEN
Apricot Chicken Breasts, 104
Baked Chicken, Lazy, 39
Baked Chicken with Corn Flake
    Crumbs, 34
Baked Fryers, 29
Barbecued Chicken, 103
California Chicken Divan, 102
Chicken Breasts in Marsala Wine, 103
Chicken Diable, 39
Chicken Fat, 11
Chicken or Beef Chow Mein, 102
Chicken, Four-Way (Israeli Style), 35
Chinese Chicken Breast with Vegetables,
    36
Crispy Chicken, Easy, 35
Curried Chicken, 103
Herb Chicken, Garden Fresh, 34
Israeli Chicken, 39
Matzo Meal Coating for Roast Chicken,
    83
Microwave Coq Au Vin (Chicken), 102
Oven Baked Chicken, 102
Roast Chicken, 22
Roast Chicken, 83
Roast Chicken with Rice, 13
Roast Turkey or Chicken, 12
Stir-Fry Chicken in Wine Sauce, 103

COOKIES

Anise Drops, 136
Apple Crisp, 122
Apple Crunch, Crispy, 78
Applesauce Cookies, 134
Apricot Squares, 135
Bon Bon Cookies, 134
Brown Sugar Cookies, 24
Brown Sugar Cookies #2, 25
Brown Sugar Pecan Rounds, 74
Brownies, 69
Brownies, Light, 70
Buttermilk Cookies, 132
Carrot Cookies, 25
Chocolate Chip Bars, 27
Chocolate Chip Bars, 133
Chocolate Chip Cookies, 19
Chocolate Chip Cookies, 76
Chocolate Fudge, Favorite, 16
Cinnamon Frosted Zucchini Bars, 70
Cinnamon Twists, 58
Cocoa Brownies, 69
Cocoa Drop Cookies, 73
Congo Squares, 71
Corn Meal Cookies, 74
Cottage Cheese Cookies, 134
Crescent Nut Cookies, 137
Date Bars, 27
Date Bars, 71
Fruit Bars, 134
Fruit or Lemon Squares, 121
Fudgies (No Bake Cookies), 133
Gingersnap Cookies, 74
Grape Vine Rolls, 90
Hanukkah Cookies, 72
Jelly Roll, 6
Jelly Roll (Sponge), 6
Kicklach (Puffy Egg Cookies), 5
Lemon Curd Squares, 120
M and M Cookies, 77
Macaroons, Easy, 132

Marshmallow Candy, 5
Meringues or Kisses, 87
Oatmeal Cookies, Famous, 75
Oatmeal Coolies, Peek-A-Boo, 73
Oatmeal Crisps, 72
Oil Pastry, 58
Old-Fashioned Rocks, 133
Old-Time Cinnamon Jumbles, 75
Peanut Butter Balls, 76
Peanut Butter Candy, 122
Peanut Butter Cookies, 74
Pecan Balls, 28
Pecan Tarts, 131
Pinwheel Cookies, 72
Poppy Seed Cookies, Famous, 22
Puffs, Small "Duchess", 96
Rocky Road Bars, 32
Sesame Cookies, 133
Snowflakes, 4
Soft Molasses Cookies, 136
Sweet Rolls, 6
Tutti Frutti Squares, 71
Walnut Snack, 52
Washboard Cookies, 76
Yum Yums, 97

DRINKS

Grape Juice Fresh From Garden, Home-Made, 54
Punch #2, Champagne, 93
Punch, Champagne, 93
Punch, Cold Duck, 94
Punch, Green Colored, 56
Punch, Open-House, 55
Punch, Southern Comfort, 94
Punch, Thoenen's, 56
Sea Breeze Drink, 94
Tea Kettle Tea, 13
Tea Time Tassies, 130
Whiskey Sour, 94

EGGS, PANCAKES

Egg Drops, 82
Egg Kichlech, 118
Farfel Pancakes, 84
Matzo Meal Omelet, 86
Matzo Meal Pancakes, 84
Non-Fat Egg Rolls, 116
One-Eyed Pete, 115
Paper Thin Pancakes, 115
Roasted Eggs, 90

FISH

Baked Fish (Flounder, Sole, Haddock), 44
Baked Fish Fillets Parmesan, 109
Broiled Fish (Greek Style), 109
Broiled Salmon Steak or Fillet, 45
Broiled Trout or Whiting Fish, 45
Creamed Sole or Haddock, 44
Fillet of Sole, 24
Fish, Fabulous, 26
Fried Fish (Flounder, Haddock, Sole or Trout), 45
Gefilte Fish, 14
Orange-Lemon Halibut Steaks, 109
Paella (Mexican dish), 54
Salmon Loaf, 16
Salmon Loaf, 28
Smoked Salmon, Hot, 80
Trout in Envelopes for Two, 45
Tuna Hot Dish, 29

FROSTINGS, ICINGS, 1

Brown Sugar Meringue Frosting, 64
Butter Frosting, 70
Butter Icing, 131
Butterscotch Icing, 68
Caramel Frosting, Easy, 64
Chocolate Frosting, 132
Chocolate Frosting, 21
Chocolate Vanilla Frosting, 62

Cinnamon Frosting, 70
Cocoa Icing, 62
Cocoa Icing, Simple, 63
Coconut Frosting, 131
Cream Cheese Icing for Zucchini, Banana, and Nut Breads, 131
Creamy Chocolate Frosting, 132
Creamy Vanilla Frosting, 62
Egg Yolk Icing, 66
Fluffy White Frosting, 130
Fluffy White Frosting, 67
French Silk Frosting, 68
Fudge Icing, 62
Lemon Swirl Frosting, 79
Marie's Chocolate Icing, 69
Minute Fudge Frosting, 129
Peanut Butter Broiled Topping, 65
Peanut Butter Icing, 62
Penuche Icing, 63
Richmond Chocolate Frosting, 66
White Icing, 64

FRUIT
Freezer Raspberry and Strawberry Jams, 55
Frozen Cinnamon Apples, 96
Frozen Strawberries, Home-Made, 55
Grape Jam, 55
Orange Sherbet Dessert, 120
Pineapple Dessert, 121
Raspberry Jam, Home-Made, 55
Scalloped Apples, 96
Strawberries Romanoff, 121
Strawberry Jam, 55

LAMB
Barbecued Lamb Breast (or Beef Short-Ribs), 43
Greek Lamb with String Beans, 43
Lamb Pilaf, 42

LIVER
Chopped Liver, 11
Chopped Liver Appetizer, 94
Fried Liver in Sweet and Sour Sauce, 105
Liver Patties, 11
Pesach Meeana (Liver Dish), 9
Potato Liver Knishes, 106

PIES
Apple Pie Crust, 25
Apple Pie Filling, 25
Apple Pie, Crazy Crust, 122
Apple Strudel, 26
Blueberry Cheese Pie, 60
Blueberry Cobbler, Fresh, 58
Cherry Cream Pie, 21
Chocolate Pie, 124
Dutch Apple Pie, 123
Eggplant Pie, 88
French Apple Pie, 59
Fresh Fruit Pie, Deep Dish, 59
Hamentaschen, 77
Hamentaschen & Flacht Dough, 20
Hamentashen, 136
Ice Cream Pie, 17
Lemon Lush, 137
Lemon Meringue Pie, 124
Lemon Sponge Pie, 122
Pastry for Pie, Delicious, 123
Peach Custard Pie, 123
Pecan Pie, 33
Pecan Pie, Jessie Wallace's, 124
Pie Crust, Perfect, 122
Pumpkin Pie, 124
Pumpkin Pie, Fresh, 58
Strudel, 136

PUDDINGS
Bread Pudding, 120
Cottage Cheese Jell-O Mold, 97
Cottage Cheese Pudding, 10
Eggplant Pudding, 89
Flooden (Lena Lerner's favorite Purim dessert), 4
Lime-Sour Cream Mold, 97
Matzo Pudding, Passover, 85
Noodle Pudding, 8
Noodle Pudding, 18
Noodle Pudding, 26
Noodle Pudding, Adath, 30
Rice Pudding, 8
Rice Pudding, 113
Spinach Pudding, 89

RICE, POTATOES, PASTA
Boiled Bulgur, 111
Buckwheat Grits, 12
Chinese Fried Rice, 113
Chop Suey, Quick and Easy, 108
Kasha, 38
Kasha with Shell Macaroni, 15
Monterey Pasta, Right-Away, 48
Noodle Rice Pilaf, 113
Parsley Pareve Potatoes, 84
Potato Latkes, 54
Potato Latkes, Uncle Miltie's, 110
Potato Noodles (Shlishkas), 111
Spanish Rice (Mexican dish), 54
Spinach and Rice, 113
Stuffed Pasta Shells, 78
Sweet Potatoes Candied with Brown Sugar, 49
Zucchini with Pasta, 53

SAUCES
Applesauce, 78
Applesauce, Home-Made, 55
Baked Cranberry Sauce, 78
Chinese Sauce for Vegetables, 37
Chopped Meat Sauce for Spaghetti, 108

Peach Sauce, Fresh, 121
Sweet and Sour Sauce, 41
Tomato Sauce for Gefilte Fish, 14
Tomato Sauce, Summer, 46

SOUPS, BORSCHT
Beef Soup with Navy Beans, 15
Beeft Borscht, 11
Beeft Borscht (Dairy), 29
Beeft Borscht, Perfect (Meatless), 28
Black Bean Soup, 98
Broccoli and Zucchini Soup, 47
Cabbage Borscht, 11
Cabbage Borscht, 99
Cabbage Soup, 11
Canned Beef Borscht, 12
Chicken Soup, 12
Creamy Pumpkin Soup, 17
Lentil Soup, Easy, 91
Lettuce Soup (with Peas), 99
Pea Soup with Beef, 16
Potato Soup, 99
"Souper" Chicken, 40
Stuffed Cabbage Leaves and Cabbage Soup, 40
Toasted Farfel for Soup, 82
Tomato Soup, 100
Vegetable Soup, 99
Vegetable Soup, 99
Vichyssoise Soup, 100
Zucchini-Spaghetti Soup, 54

STUFFING
Almond-Rice Stuffing or Casserole, 112
Bread Stuffing, 24
Mushroom Stuffing, Passover, 83
Stuffing for Veal Breast, 43

VEAL
Baked Veal, Russian Style, 44
Paprika Schnitzel, 44

Stuffed Breast of Veal, 43
Veal Chops, 26
Veal Steak in Tomato Sauce, 44

VEGETABLES, LEGUMES, SALADS
Baked Beans, 23
Baked Beans, Quick, 23
Baked Onions, 100
Baked Squash, 101
Beef and Eggplant (Greek Musaca), 42
Braised Zucchini, 101
Butternut Squash, 51
Cabbage Salad, 49
Celery Knobs, 89
Charoses—Passover, 81
Chopped Onions in Mazola Oil, 13
Cole Slaw, 98
Corn and Lima Bean Chowder (Dairy), 48
Creamed Onions, 100
Crunchy Pea Salad, 98
Cucumber Salad, 52
Eggplant Appetizer, 10
Eggplant Appetizer, 90
Eggplant Parmigiana, 32
French Dressing, 28
French Dressing, 50
Frozen Vegetables with Gefilte Fish, 14
Fruit Salad, 97
Garlic Pasta Salad, 30
Givéch (Cooked vegetable salad), 22
Honey Poppy Seed Dressing, 31
Kohlrabi, 91
Leek Patties, 90
Leeks, 89
Macaroni Salad, Easy, 50
Marinated Carrots, 101
Marinated Mixed Vegetables, 100
Marinated Potato Salad, 98

Marinated Raw Mushrooms, 95
Oil Free Eggplant, 51
Pickled Beets, 100
Pickled Cabbage, 101
Pickles (Green Plum Tomatoes or Green Pickles), 21
Procas (Stuffed Cabbage Leaves), 13
Russian Fruit Salad, 95
Salad, Sunshine, 49
Scalloped Tomatoes, 51
Sliced Cucumber Pickles, 52
Sliced Cucumber Pickles, 95
Squash Fritters, 53
Stewed String Beans, 50
Stuffed Cabbage, 106
Stuffed Mushrooms, 52
Summer Squash, Sandwich Pickles, 22
Sweet and Sour Stuffed Peppers, 40
Vegetable Dip, Easy, 95
Vegetables, Beautiful Winter, 101
Zucchini Vegetable Soup, 48
Zucchini-Bean Stir-Fry, 53

Author Index (by first name!)

ANONYMOUS
Banana Muffins, 120

ADA WASSERMAN
Givéch (Cooked vegetable salad), 22

ALMUS RUSSELL
Peanut Butter Candy, 122

AUNT MERLE
Pickles (Green Plum Tomatoes or Green Pickles), 21

BARBARA BEHR
Vichyssoise Soup, 100

BARBARA ZABITZ
Tsimmes, 111

BARRY SATZ
Chili, 77

BETSY MARATECK
Baked Cheese and Egg Dish, 115

BETTY GEARINGER
Chocolate Devil's Food Cake, 125
Lemon Sponge Pie, 122
Scalloped Apples, 96

BILLIE HENRIE
Strawberries Romanoff, 121

BOB REEDER
Frankfurters and Sauerkraut, 108

CASSIE SELK
Butter Icing, 131
Chocolate Pie, 124
Crane Pumpkin Bread, 116
Fluffy White Frosting, 130
Peach Custard Pie, 123
Pie Crust, Perfect, 122
Rice Pudding, 113
Vegetable Soup, 99

CONNIE FROHMAN
Anise Drops, 136
Chicken Breasts in Marsala Wine, 103
Corn and Broccoli Casserole, 110
Curried Chicken, 103
Danish Meat Balls, 107
Frozen Cinnamon Apples, 96
Processor Orange Bread, 117
Punch #2, Champagne, 93
Rice Cakes, 112
Vegetable Dip, Easy, 95

DEBORAH POPLAWSKY
Fruit or Lemon Squares, 121

DINAH ELKIN
Baked Fryers, 29
Beet Borscht (Dairy), 29
Beet Borscht, Perfect (Meatless), 28
Garlic Pasta Salad, 30
Honey Cake, 31
Honey Poppy Seed Dressing, 31
Meat Loaf, 31
Noodle Pudding, Adath, 30
Pear Cake, 30
Rocky Road Bars, 32
Tuna Hot Dish, 29

Zucchini Casserole, 29
Zucchini-Pineapple Bread, 32

DOC ASH
Punch, Southern Comfort, 94

DOROTHY WILSON
Soft Molasses Cookies, 136

DOTTIE HALFMANN
Rib Roast of Beef, 104

EDITHA GRIFFITH
Baked Onions, 100
Creamed Onions, 100

ELEANOR SHAMIS
Apple Crisp, 122
Fruit Salad, 97
Lasagna, 107

ELISABETH HENRIE
Apple Pie, Crazy Crust, 122
Black Bean Soup, 98

ESTHER FALK
Potato Noodles (Shlishkas), 111

ESTHER LERNER
Apple Cake, 18
Chocolate Chip Cookies, 19
Kamesh Brot, 19
Mandel Bread, 19
Roast Brisket or Chuck Roast, 20
Roast Chicken, 22
Spinach Kugel, 19

ESTHER ZABITZ
Blintzes, 114
Cheese Pit, Eleanor Deutsh's, 114
Mandelbrot, 135
Pickled Beets, 100
Potato Latkes, Uncle Miltie's, 110
Russian Fruit Salad, 95

ETHEL "TOOTS" LERNER
Marble Coffee Cake, 18
Noodle Pudding, 18

FAN GOLDMAN
Cheese Blintzes, 27
Chocolate Chip Bars, 27
Date Bars, 27

Fish, Fabulous, 26
French Dressing, 28
Noodle Pudding, 26
Pecan Balls, 28
Salmon Loaf, 28

FANNIE GOLDMAN
Veal Chops, 26

FAY HOLLISTER
Pumpkin Bread, 118

GERRY ROMEO
Ricotta Cake, 126

GERRY ROMERO
Sesame Cookies, 133

HAROLD ARNOW
Punch, Cold Duck, 94

HELEEN GREENWALD
Eggplant Appetizer, 90

HELEN COLLEN
Apple Crumb Cake, 127
Prune Nut Cake, 128

HELEN MILLER
Minute Fudge Frosting, 129
Puffs, Small "Duchess", 96
Wet Chocolate Cake, 129

IDA FATTMAN
Blueberry Cake, 126
Chocolate Chip Bars, 133

IRIS LEVY
Cream Cheese Icing for Zucchini,
   Banana, and Nut Breads, 131

JANET STAMM
Vegetable Soup, 99

JEAN REED
Chop Suey, Quick and Easy, 108
Chopped Liver Appetizer, 94
Creamy Chocolate Frosting, 132
Dark Chocolate Cupcakes, 130
Lemon Meringue Pie, 124
One-Eyed Pete, 115
Paper Thin Pancakes, 115

JEAN SHERMAN
Carrot Cake, 127

JENNIE HASSON
Coconut Frosting, 131
Fruit Cocktail Cake, 127

JOAN SATZ
Eggplant Parmigiana, 32
Pecan Pie, 33

JOANNA BUCKINGHAM
Buttermilk Cookies, 132

JOHN BAIRD
Whiskey Sour, 94

JUDIE HIRSHFIELD
Microwave Coq Au Vin (Chicken), 102

JUDITH BRANDT
Non-Fat Egg Rolls, 116

JUDY WEINBERG
Broiled Fish (Greek Style), 109
Chinese Fried Rice, 113

KATHERINE NAGEL
Orange Sherbet Dessert, 120

KATHLEEN HINKEL
Marinated Carrots, 101

LENA LERNER
Beef Soup with Navy Beans, 15
Beet Borscht, 11
Blintzes, 14
Bread Rolls, 6
Buckwheat Grits, 12
Cabbage Borscht, 11
Cabbage Soup, 11
Canned Beet Borscht, 12
Cheese Bagalach, 7
Cheese Rolls, Famous, 8
Chicken Fat, 11
Chicken Soup, 12
Chopped Liver, 11
Chopped Onions in Mazola Oil, 13
Cottage Cheese Dumplings, 10
Cottage Cheese Pudding, 10
Eggplant Appetizer, 10
Flooden (Lena Lerner's favorite Purim dessert), 4
Frozen Vegetables with Gefilte Fish, 14
Gefilte Fish, 14
Ground Beef with Macaroni, 15

Hamburger Patties (Lena Lerner's Specialty), 9
Honey Cake #2, 7
Honey Cake, 5
Ice Cream Pie, 17
Jelly Roll (Sponge), 6
Jelly Roll, 6
Kamesh Bread, 5
Kasha with Shell Macaroni, 15
Kicklach (Puffy Egg Cookies), 5
Kneidlach (Matzo Balls), 9
Kreplach, 10
Liver Patties, 11
Macaroni and Cheese Dish, Easy, 14
Mamaliga—Cheese and Butter, 9
Marshmallow Candy, 5
Noodle Pudding, 8
Oatmeal Pancakes, 11
Pea Soup with Beef, 16
Pesach Meeana (Liver Dish), 9
Pesach Popovers, 8
Procas (Stuffed Cabbage Leaves), 13
Rice Pudding, 8
Roast Beef, 13
Roast Chicken with Rice, 13
Roast Turkey or Chicken, 12
Rolled Roast, 12
Salmon Loaf, 16
Snowflakes, 4
Sweet Rolls, 6
Tea Kettle Tea, 13
Tomato Sauce for Gefilte Fish, 14

LIBBY RUDNIK
Bread Pudding, 120
Marinated Mixed Vegetables, 100

LIL BELL
Chocolate Cake, 20
Chocolate Frosting, 21
Hamentaschen & Flacht Dough, 20
Mondel Bread, 20

LISA MAEL
Challah, Never-Fail, 119
Vegetables, Beautiful Winter, 101

LIZ KINSLINGER
Rhubarb Crunch Coffee Cake, 118

LIZ STURGEON
Old-Fashioned Rocks, 133

LOIS STURGEON
Applesauce Cookies, 134
Bean Casserole, Fresh, 110
Beef and Rice Bake, 106
Chocolate Chip Coffee Cake, 119
Cole Slaw, 98
Fruit Bars, 134
Fudgies (No Bake Cookies), 133
Lettuce Soup (with Peas), 99
Marinated Potato Salad, 98

LOUISE MITRANI
Eggplant Pie, 88
Roasted Eggs, 90
Zucchini Squash and Cheese Casserole, 89

MABEL ASH
Cheese Straws, 94
Yum Yums, 97

MADELYN SATZ
Baked Cranberry Sauce, 78
Carrot Cake, 79
Cream Cheese Swirl Frosting, 79
Spicy Rhubarb Cake, 79
Spicy Zucchini Cake, 79
Stuffed Pasta Shells, 78

MARGE LERNER
Chocolate Fudge, Favorite, 16

MARIAN CABELLY
Baked Fish Fillets Parmesan, 109
Matzo Meal Coating for Roast Chicken, 83
Noodle Kugel, Mrs. Kantor's Fabulous, 112
Noodle Rice Pilaf, 113
Orange-Lemon Halibut Steaks, 109
Stir-Fry Chicken in Wine Sauce, 103

MARY GLUCHOFF
Cabbage Borscht, 99
Egg Kichlech, 118
Matzo Charlotte—Passover, 84
Stuffed Cabbage, 106

MARY NOLL
Cream Cheese Cupcakes, 130
Crunchy Pea Salad, 98
Tea Time Tassies, 130
Vegetable Casserole, 110

MARY STURGEON
Marinated Raw Mushrooms, 95

MARY WRIGHT
Cottage Cheese Jell-O Mold, 97
Garlic Crackers (dairy), 96
Macaroons, Easy, 132
Peach Sauce, Fresh, 121
Pound Cake, Poor Man's, 126

MATTIE HASSON
Spinach and Rice, 113

MAXINE ARNOW
Matzo Meal Blintzes, 85
Matzo Pudding, Passover, 85
Mushroom Stuffing, Passover, 83

MICHAEL KOJIS
Smoked Salmon, Hot, 80

MIRIAM LERNER SATZ
"Souper" Chicken, 40
Apple Cake, Jewish, 61
Apple Coffee Cake, 61
Applesauce, Home-Made, 55
Bagels, Passover, 84
Baked Chicken with Corn Flake
    Crumbs, 34
Baked Chicken, Lazy, 39
Baked Fish (Flounder, Sole,
    Haddock), 44
Baked Veal, Russian Style, 44
Banana Bread, 56
Banana-Nut Cake, 68
Barbecued Lamb Breast (or Beef
    Short-Ribs), 43
Beef and Eggplant (Greek Musaca), 42
Blintz Torte, 66
Blueberry Cheese Pie, 60
Blueberry Cobbler, Fresh, 58
Blueberry-Cheesecake Dessert, 60
Bonnie Butter Cake, 68
Brisket, 37
Broccoli and Zucchini Soup, 47

Broccoli Casserole, 51
Broiled Salmon Steak or Fillet, 45
Broiled Trout or Whiting Fish, 45
Brown Sugar Meringue Frosting, 64
Brown Sugar Pecan Rounds, 74
Brownies, 69
Brownies, Light, 70
Butter Frosting, 70
Butternut Squash, 51
Butterscotch Icing, 68
Cabbage Salad, 49
Caramel Frosting, Easy, 64
Chafing Dish Meatballs, 42
Charoses—Passover, 81
Cheese Cake, 60
Chicken Diable, 39
Chicken, Everybody's Favorite, 35
Chicken, Four-Way (Israeli Style), 35
Chili Con Carne, 40
Chinese Chicken Breast with
    Vegetables, 36
Chinese Sauce for Vegetables, 37
Chocolate Cake #2, Wacky, 64
Chocolate Cake, 63
Chocolate Cake, Wacky, 63
Chocolate Chip Cookies, 76
Chocolate Vanilla Frosting, 62
Chuck Roast, 36
Cinnamon Frosted Zucchini Bars, 70
Cinnamon Frosting, 70
Cinnamon Twists, 58
Cocoa Brownies, 69
Cocoa Drop Cookies, 73
Cocoa Icing, 62
Cocoa Icing, Simple, 63
Congo Squares, 71
Corn and Lima Bean Chowder
    (Dairy), 48
Corn Meal Cookies, 74
Cottage Cheese and Noodle Dish,
    Easy, 47
Creamed Sole or Haddock, 44
Creamy Vanilla Frosting, 62
Crispy Chicken, Easy, 35
Cucumber Salad, 52
Date Bars, 71
Dinette Cake, 66

Egg Drops, 82
Egg Yolk Icing, 66
Farfel Pancakes, 84
Fikonicas (Greek-Style Cholent), 37
Fluffy White Frosting, 67
Freezer Raspberry and Strawerry
    Jams, 55
French Apple Pie, 59
French Dressing, 50
French Silk Frosting, 68
Fresh Fruit Pie, Deep Dish, 59
Fried Fish (Flounder, Haddock,
    Sole or Trout), 45
Frozen Strawberries, Home-Made, 55
Fudge Icing, 62
Gingersnap Cookies, 74
Golden Layer Cake, Best All
    Around Cake, 61
Grape Jam, 55
Grape Juice Fresh From Garden,
    Home-Made, 54
Greek Lamb with String Beans, 43
Ground Beef Macaroni Casserole, 42
Hanukkah Cookies, 72
Hawaiian Pineapple Cake, 67
Herb Chicken, Garden Fresh, 34
Israeli Chicken, 39
Italian Spaghetti and Meat Balls, 38
Kasha, 38
Lamb Pilaf, 42
London Broil in a Wok, 37
London Broil, 36
M and M Cookies, 77
Macaroni Salad, Easy, 50
Marble Cake, 62
Marie's Chocolate Icing, 69
Matzo Balls, Best, 82
Matzo Brie (Fried Matzo), 81
Matzo Meal Omelet, 86
Matzo Meal Pancakes, 84
Meringues or Kisses, 87
Monterey Pasta, Right-Away, 48
New York Frankfurters, 38
Oatmeal Cookies, Famous, 75
Oatmeal Cookies, Peek-A-Boo, 73
Oatmeal Crisps, 72
Oatmeal Spice Cake, 65

Oil Free Eggplant, 51
Oil Pastry, 58
Old-Time Cinnamon Jumbles, 75
Paella (Mexican dish), 54
Paprika Schnitzel, 44
Parsley Pareve Potatoes, 84
Peanut Butter Balls, 76
Peanut Butter Broiled Topping, 65
Peanut Butter Cookies, 74
Peanut Butter Icing, 62
Penuche Icing, 63
Pineapple Zucchini Bread, 57
Pinwheel Cookies, 72
Popovers, Best Passover, 82
Potato Latkes, 54
Pumpkin Pie, Fresh, 58
Punch, Green Colored, 56
Punch, Open-House, 55
Punch, Thoenen's, 56
Raspberry Jam, Home-Made, 55
Richmond Chocolate Frosting, 66
Roast Chicken, 83
Rolled Roast, 36
Russian Meat Balls, 39
Salad, Sunshine, 49
Scalloped Tomatoes, 51
Sliced Cucumber Pickles, 52
Spanish Rice (Mexican dish), 54
Spice Cake, Quick-Method, 64
Squash Fritters, 53
Stewed String Beans, 50
Strawberry Jam, 55
Stuffed Breast of Veal, 43
Stuffed Cabbage Leaves and
    Cabbage Soup, 40
Stuffed Mushrooms, 52
Stuffed Zucchini with Ground
    Beef, 41
Stuffing for Veal Breast, 43
Sweet and Sour Sauce, 41
Sweet and Sour Stuffed Peppers, 40
Sweet Potatoes Candied with
    Brown Sugar, 49
Toasted Farfel for Soup, 82
Tomato Sauce, Summer, 46
Trout in Envelopes for Two, 45
Tuna Bread, Hot, 45

Tuna, Noodle, and Mushroom
    Soup Casserole, 46
Tutti Frutti Squares, 71
Veal Steak in Tomato Sauce, 44
Walnut Snack, 52
Washboard Cookies, 76
White Cake with Grated
    Chocolate (Ski Cake), 65
White Icing, 64
Zucchini Bread, 56
Zucchini Muffins, 57
Zucchini Vegetable Soup, 48
Zucchini Walnut Bread, 56
Zucchini with Pasta, 53
Zucchini-Bean Stir-Fry, 53
Zucchini-Spaghetti Soup, 54

MIRIAM REISMAN
    Chinese Steak, 104
    Chopped Meat Sauce for Spaghetti,
    108
    Fried Liver in Sweet and Sour
        Sauce, 105
    Poppy Seed Cake, 125

MOLLY SCARPINO
    California Chicken Divan, 102

MONICA ALLEN
    Chili, 105

MOTHER SATZ
    Apple Pie Crust, 25
    Apple Pie Filling, 25
    Apple Strudel, 26
    Baked Beans, 23
    Baked Beans, Quick, 23
    Bread Stuffing, 24
    Brown Sugar Cookies #2, 25
    Brown Sugar Cookies, 24
    Carrot Cookies, 25
    Chuck Stew, 24
    Fillet of Sole, 24
    Meat Loaf, Famous, 23
    Poppy Seed Cookies, Famous, 22
    Taglach Dumplings, 24

NAOMI HESKEL
    Almond-Rice Stuffing or
        Casserole, 112

Boiled Bulgur, 111
Bon Bon Cookies, 134
Braised Zucchini, 101
Challah Sabbath Twists, 117

NINA FELDSER
    Cheese Cake, 125
    Lemon Curd Squares, 120

PATTY MOSIER
    Sea Breeze Drink, 94

PEG WOZNEK
    Apricot Chicken Breasts, 104

RANDY KRAUSS
    Dairy Kugel, 111

RAZIE ABRAMS
    Dutch Apple Pie, 123

REINA BAKISH
    Apple Nut Cake, 138
    Lemon Lush, 137

ROSE BAKISH
    Barbecued Ground Beef, 107
    Boiled Tongue, 105
    Buttermilk Cake, 128
    Celery Knobs, 89
    Cheesies, 91
    Crescent Nut Cookies, 137
    Eggplant Pudding, 89
    Flanken (Short Ribs), 104
    Grape Vine Rolls, 90
    Green Tomatoes with Ground Beef, 92
    Kohlrabi, 91
    Leek Patties, 90
    Leeks, 89
    Lentil Soup, Easy, 91
    Meat-Spinach Soufflé, 88
    Moussaka (Eastern Casserole), 88
    Oven Baked Chicken, 102
    Pineapple Dessert, 121
    Pumpkin Pie, 124
    Sour Cream Nut Cake, 92
    Spinach Pudding, 89
    Spinach-Meat Patties, 90

RUBY LEE
    Cherry Cream Cheese Topped Cake, 128
    Raisin Cake, 129

RUTH GOLDBERG
  Summer Squash, Sandwich Pickles, 22

RUTH SCHWIMMER
  Chicken or Beef Chow Mein, 102
  Funnel Cakes, Amish, 115
  Hamentashen, 136

SANDY DAVIS
  Creamy Pumpkin Soup, 17

SARA AND EVE KRAUSS
  Sliced Cucumber Pickles, 95

SELMA MITRANI
  Pecan Pie, Jessie Wallace's, 124

SONIA FISHER
  Pickled Cabbage, 101
  Potato Soup, 99

SOPHIE BRAEMAN
  Cherry Cream Pie, 21

STEPHANIE CHERNIAK
  Apple Crunch, Crispy, 78
  Hamentaschen, 77
  Noodle-Vegetable Cheese Casserole, 77

STEPHEN CHERNIAK
  Applesauce, 78

SUSAN KOFF
  Baked Squash, 101
  Quiche Lorraine, 114

TOM STURGEON
  Punch, Champagne, 93

VIVIENNE ARCUS
  Apricot Squares, 135
  Barbecued Chicken, 103

Chocolate Frosting, 132
Cottage Cheese Cookies, 134
Frankfurter and Bean Casserole, 108
Honey and Nut Cake, 126
Lime-Sour Cream Mold, 97
Mohn (Poppy Seed) Shortbread, 118
Nut Torte, 128
Pastry for Pie, Delicious, 123
Pecan Tarts, 131
Potato Liver Knishes, 106
Sponge Cake, Best Passover, 86
Strudel, 136
Tomato Soup, 100

"Keeping alive these simple treasures is the purpose of *Heirloom Cookbook.* May the recipes it contains add to the enjoyment at many tables on many occasions."

—Miriam Lerner Satz